CULTURE SMART!
THAILAND

Roger Jones

Graphic Arts Center Publishing®

First published in Great Britain 2003
by Kuperard, an imprint of Bravo Ltd.

Series Editor Geoffrey Chesler
Design DW Design

Simultaneously published in the U.S.A. and Canada
by Graphic Arts Center Publishing Company
P. O. Box 10306, Portland, OR 97296-0306

Third printing 2006

Library of Congress Cataloging-in-Publication Data

Jones, Roger (Roger Alan), 1942-
Thailand : a quick guide to culture and etiquette / Roger Jones.
     p. cm. — (Culture smart!)
Includes bibliographical references and index.
ISBN 1-55868-778-5 (softbound)
1. Thailand—Social life and customs. 2. Etiquette—Thailand. 3.
National characteristics, Thai. I. Title. II. Series.
DS568.J66 2003
959.3--dc22

                                   2003019212

Printed in Malaysia

Cover image: Wat Mongkol Nimit, Phuket Island.
Travel Ink/Simon Reddy

About the Author

ROGER JONES is a lecturer and writer specializing in careers, living and working abroad, and classical music. After graduating from King's College, London University, he worked in education for extended periods in many countries around the world, including several years in Thailand and Cambodia. He has written eight handbooks, including *Teaching Abroad*, *Getting a Job Abroad*, *How to Master Languages*, *Retire Abroad*, and *How to Manage Your Career*. He is a member of the Career Writers' Association and the Society of Authors, and was formerly a member of the Chartered Institute of Management and the Institute of Administrative Management.

Other Books in the Series

Other titles are in preparation. For more information, contact: info@kuperard.co.uk

The publishers would like to thank **CultureSmart!**Consulting for its help in researching and developing the concept for this series.

contents

contents

Map of Thailand

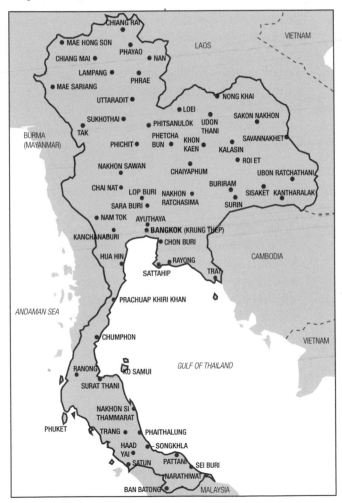

introduction

To most outsiders Thailand represents the East at
its most mysterious and enigmatic. While on the
surface Bangkok looks like many other modern
cities, when you start to interact with the locals
differences emerge. Thais react in surprising and
unexpected ways. They giggle when you get
angry; they get upset if you touch them; they
flatter you when it is completely unjustified; and
in the most stressful situations they never seem to
lose their cool. You seek to probe beneath the
surface and they smile and become inscrutable.

Although the Thais seem charming, gentle, and
tolerant, not every visitor feels at ease when
dealing with them. Outsiders sometimes deplore
their passivity, dislike the fact that they do not
give direct answers, or get irritated by their
apparent smugness. However, Thai behavior is
rooted in the way they view the world, which is
influenced by their beliefs, culture, and traditions.

Thais put a great deal of effort into social skills
in order to maintain social harmony. They seek to
avoid confrontation at all costs, since this only
causes unpleasantness and potential loss of face
for all parties. But not everything is what it seems.
One of the Thais' most potent weapons is the
smile that puts people at ease and helps to defuse
difficult situations. On the other hand, it may also
serve to cover up feelings or thoughts they do not

wish to divulge, or to indicate that there is nothing more to be said on a subject. There are also times when the veneer of charm can turn out to be paper-thin—when you have a brush with authority, for instance. Whether you are visting Thailand on business or for pleasure, you need to be aware that different rules and standards apply.

Even if you are planning to stay for only a short while, you will find your experience enriched if you make an effort to understand the people and to blend in with their lifestyle. As a guest in their country, you will be made to feel at home—all the more reason not to abuse this hospitality by behaving in a manner they might find offensive.

I make no apologies for including extended sections on history, religion, and the Thai monarchy in this short book, for I believe it is impossible to comprehend the Thai psyche without such background knowledge. Thailand has a long and rich culture that continues to be a potent influence even in modern times.

A final word about spelling. In Thai names *ph* is an aspirated *p* (not *f*), *th* is an aspirated *t*, and *kh* an aspirated *k*. In words transliterated for the purposes of this book the *h* is omitted. Thai official spelling is used for names, places, and festivals; otherwise phonetic spelling easily understood by English speakers is used.

Key Facts

Official name	Kingdom of Thailand	*Prathet Thai* (Land of the Free)
Capital City	Bangkok: population 10 million	*Krung Thep* (City of Celestial Beings)
Major cities	Chiang Mai, Had Yai Korat, Khon Kaen, Nakhon Si Thammarat, Ubon	
Area	198,114 sq. miles (513,115 sq. km.)	
Climate	Tropical	
Population	64 million	Per capita GDP $1806
Ethnic Make-up	Thai: 80 %, Chinese: 12%, Malay: 4%, Others: 4%.	
Language	Thai. Other languages spoken: Malay, Chinese, Khmer, Mon.	Tribal languages: Akha, Meo, Karen, etc. Principal foreign language: English
Religion	Buddhism: 94%	Islam: 4.5% Others: 1.5%
Calendar	The Thais use two calendars: Gregorian and Buddhist. The Thai Buddhist calendar is 543 years in advance of the Gregorian calendar.	
Government	A constitutional monarchy with a parliament consisting of a 200-member Senate and a 500-member House of Representatives, both elected by universal suffrage. The country is divided into 76 provinces.	

Currency	*Baht*	Coins: 1,5,10 Baht Notes: B10 (brown), B20 (green), B50 (blue), B100 (red), B 500 (purple), B1,000 (gray)
Media	The leading broadsheet Thai language newspaper is *Siam Rath*. The popular press includes *Thai Rath* and the *Daily News*.	
Media: English Language	The main English-language newspapers are the *Bangkok Post* and *The Nation*.	
Business Hours	9:00 a.m. to 5:00 p.m. Monday to Friday, except public holidays.	
Banking Hours	9:30 a.m. to 3:30 p.m. Monday to Friday, except public holidays	
Electricity	220 Volt AC 50 cycles.	Most sockets are two-prong.
Video/TV	The PAL system is in use.	
Telephone	The country code is 66.	To call abroad from Thailand dial 00.
Local Time	GMT + 7 hours	

chapter one

LAND & PEOPLE

Thailand was known as Siam until 1939, when it was changed to *Muang Thai* or *Prathet Thai*, which both mean "Land of the Free." After World War II it reverted to Siam for a short period, but became Thailand again in 1949.

It is roughly the size of France and shaped like a tall tree leaning to the right. Thai school children are taught to describe the shape of their country as an elephant's head with a long dangling trunk. It is bordered to the west and northwest by Burma (Myanmar), to the northeast by Laos, to the east by Cambodia, and to the south by Malaysia, the Gulf of Thailand, and the Andaman Sea.

THE REGIONS OF THAILAND

The Central Plain
This is a huge and mostly flat alluvial plain on which Bangkok stands and where a large proportion of Thailand's rice crop is grown. The

hub of the plain is Bangkok, with the twin city of Thonburi across the river (together they are known as Metropolitan Bangkok).

Metropolitan Bangkok is an enormous, sprawling city of approximately 10 million that has expanded rapidly over the past forty years. All other Thai cities are minnows in comparison. Like many other Third World cities, it is a magnet for the rural poor, and there are extremes of wealth and poverty. It suffers from a weak infrastructure, appalling pollution, and gridlocked traffic.

Other important centers are Kanchanaburi, Nakorn Pathom, Rayong, Samut Songkhram, and Petchaburi, and the resorts of Pattaya and Bang Saen. The population of the central plain minus Bangkok is 14 million.

The North
This is the most scenic part of Thailand, full of mountains and hills. Chiang Mai, Phrae, Sukhothai, and Lampang are the main towns, and the region is home to various hill tribes that are ethnically and culturally different from the Thais. The northern dialect differs in some respects from the Thai spoken in the central plains, and is akin to that spoken in the Shan states of Burma. In former

times most of this area formed the early Thai
Kingdom of Lanna. Population: 17 million.

The Northeast

The Korat plateau is generally regarded as the
poorest part of Thailand, and it has less rainfall
than other parts of the country. The chief towns are
Khon Kaen, Udon Thani (Korat), Nong Khai, Roi
Et, and Ubon. The Mekhong River forms a natural
border with Laos, and the northeastern Isarn Thai
dialect is similar to Lao. Population: 21 million.

Peninsular or Southern Thailand

This region stretches down from Phetchaburi to
the Malaysian border and is only twenty-five
miles wide at its narrowest point. It is
characterized by lush vegetation and toward the
south there are tin and rubber plantations. There
are a number of holiday islands off the coast, such
as Ko Samui and Phuket. Ranong, Surat Thani,
Nakhon Si Thammarat, Songkhla, and the railway
junction of Had Yai are the important towns.
Population: 8 million.

CLIMATE AND SEASONS

Thailand has a tropical climate with three main
seasons: the hot season (March to May), the rainy
season (June to September), and the cool season

(October to February). "Cool" and "rainy" are relative terms. The average temperature in Bangkok in December is 77°F (25°C), but it usually feels much hotter because of high humidity, and there are plenty of fine days in the rainy season.

The climate varies according to location. In the mountains of the north the nights can be cold in December and January. In October severe flooding is likely to occur all over Thailand, especially in Bangkok. Areas close to the sea often suffer from high levels of humidity.

Peninsular Thailand has less sharply differentiated seasons. The southwestern coast and hills experience the full force of the southwestern monsoon between May and October, while on the eastern side most rain falls between October and December.

THE PEOPLE
Although there is some ethnic diversity in Thailand, the proportions of which are debatable, over 99 percent of Thai residents have Thai citizenship and most of them identify closely with the country of their birth.

The Thais
The Thai people are believed to have originated in the Altai mountain region of northern Mongolia

5,000 years ago. They emigrated westward to the Yellow River and later to the mouth of the Huang Ho River and the Chinese province of Szechuan. Attacks by the Tatars and Chinese drove them further south, and by the first century CE they were living in the Yunnan Valley of south central China. In the seventh century CE they began to move southward, settling in what is now Laos and northern Thailand, and gradually absorbed the indigenous Mon and Khmer inhabitants.

The Chinese

Much of the commercial life of the country is in the hands of the Chinese, some of whom have been here since the eighteenth century, have intermarried with Thais, and have adopted Thai ways. There were also waves of Chinese immigrants in the nineteenth and twentieth centuries, a minority of whom still practice their own traditions (such as Confucianism). They account for between 11 and 14 percent of the population.

The Malays

This is the third-largest ethnic group. They practice Islam, speak Malay and Thai, and live in the four southern provinces of Narathiwat, Pattani, Yala, and Satun. Some have settled in Bangkok and other cities.

The Khmer

Together with the Mon these were the original inhabitants of Thailand who were later almost entirely assimilated by the Thais. However, Khmer (Cambodian) is spoken in the areas bordering Cambodia, and you may meet Cambodians who fled their country during the upheavals of the 1970s and '80s and did not return.

The Mon

The Mon have been almost completely assimilated by the Thais, but a few Mon-speaking communities remain in the central plain and some of the provinces.

The Indians

In the towns and cities you will find a number of Indian shopkeepers, often involved in tailoring and the textile trade. Indians are also employed as guards and night watchmen. Thai criminals are afraid of them because of their dark skins.

The Hill Tribes

There are a number of different peoples (including the Akha, Meo, Karen, Lawa, Lisu, and Hmong) who live mainly in the hills to the north and west. They are thought to number approximately 750,000, and each tribe has its own distinctive customs and languages.

THAILAND: A BRIEF HISTORY

The Early Kingdoms

In the seventh century CE the Thais began to move south into what is now Laos and northern Thailand, areas populated by the Khmers and the Mon. There was some conflict with the Khmers but the Mon kingdoms, known as Dvaravati, were more readily assimilated. The first substantial Thai kingdoms to be founded were those of Lanna, or Lannathai, under King Mengrai (1259–1317) in the north, and to its south, Sukhothai (1240–1376), whose most famous leader was King Ramkhamhaeng (1275–98).

Under King Ramkhamhaeng, Sukhothai expanded rapidly and is believed to have occupied territory stretching from Luang Prabang (now in Laos) in the north to Nakhorn Si Thammarat in the south, but excluding all lands to the east of the Chao Phraya River. Sukhothai became a great center for Thai art and architecture as well as for Theravada Buddhism. The king, who is credited with adapting the Khmer and Mon alphabets to the requirements of the Thai language, seems to have been a just and benevolent ruler, in contrast to some of the god-kings of the Khmer Empire.

> *In the time of King Ramkhamhaeng this land of Sukhothai is thriving. There is fish in the water and rice in the fields. The King has hung a bell in the opening of the gate over there. If any commoner has a grievance which sickens his belly and agonizes his heart, he goes and strikes the bell. The King questions the man, examines the case and decides it justly for him.*
> **Inscription in Thai, ascribed to King Ramkhamhaeng**

After King Ramkhamhaeng's death Sukhothai appears to have gone into a slow decline and was eventually incorporated into the Kingdom of Ayuthaya, fifty-five miles north of present-day Bangkok. Ayuthaya had been founded in 1350 by U Thong, a general of Chinese descent, who married into the Thai aristocracy. U Thong and his successors adopted many of the administrative practices of the Khmer.

Ayuthaya consolidated its grip on the former Mon kingdoms, but the Lanna kingdom remained free of Ayuthayan control. In the fifteenth century the Burmese conquered Ayuthaya, which was now coming to be known as Siam, and many of its residents were taken as slaves. There were also incursions by the Khmer at this time. Under King Naresuan (1590–1605) the Burmese were repelled, although they were to remain a constant threat, and large swathes of Cambodia came under Siamese control.

In the early seventeenth century Ayuthaya opened links with the West, sending an embassy to the Hague in 1608, and signing a treaty with Portugal soon after. Thereafter trade developed with other European countries as well as China, India, and Persia, and it became an important commercial center. Foreigners began to settle and establish businesses in the Kingdom, the population of which was estimated to be 300,000 or more in the middle of the seventeenth century—larger than London or Paris—and comprised forty different nationalities.

King Narai (1656–88) appointed as his prime minister Constantine Phaulkon, a Greek who had served in the British East India Company. Other foreigners were also given jobs in the King's service, including the Englishman Samuel White, nicknamed "Siamese" White. Embassies were exchanged with France; the French established a garrison at what is now Bangkok and provided mercenaries for the King's army. French missionaries tried in vain to convert King Narai.

After King Narai's death the French garrisons were expelled and there was a backlash against all foreigners. For the next one hundred and fifty years Siam had little contact with the West. There were regular conflicts, in particular with the Burmese, who in 1767 destroyed the capital of Ayuthaya (you can still see the ruins) and caused devastation all over the country.

This was undoubtedly Siam's darkest hour. However, Phya Taksin, who had come to Ayuthaya to be invested as Governor of Kampaengpet Province, managed to escape with five hundred men and set about wresting the country from the Burmese. Taksin was invited to become King and he established a new capital at Thonburi on the opposite bank of the Chao Phraya River to where Bangkok now stands. During his reign (1768–82) he not only succeeded in driving back the Burmese, but also led successful military campaigns in Burma and Laos.

King Taksin became mentally unbalanced, and was forced to abdicate in favor of one of his generals, Chao Phya Chakri (Rama I), who moved the Siamese capital across the river to Bangkok and founded a royal dynasty that has continued until the present day.

The Nineteenth and Twentieth Centuries

During the first decades of the Chakri dynasty there was further conflict between Siam and her neighbors as well as the Vietnamese. During this time much of western Cambodia was brought under Siamese control, including the former capital of the Khmer Empire, Angkor. At this time the northern Lannathai kingdom, which had at various times been independent or a vassal state, became fully incorporated into Siam.

By the beginning of the third decade of the nineteenth century a new threat to Siamese independence arose in the form of the European colonial powers. The Siamese were eventually forced to concede territory they held in Cambodia and Laos to the French, and four of the southern Malay states to Britain. However, most of the country remained intact, thanks to the skillful diplomacy of successive kings and their officials (see Chapter 4, Monarchy and Military).

The Siamese were open to Western ideas and adopted Western technology with great enthusiasm, and by the beginning of the twentieth century Siam had all the trappings of a modern state. It became a player on the world stage when it supported the Allies in World War I, sending troops to fight in northern France. After the war the country was to become one of the founding members of the League of Nations.

In 1932 the absolute monarchy came to an end after a bloodless coup—the first of eighteen in the twentieth century—by a group of "Young Turks" led by Pridi Phanamyong and Phraya Phahon Phonpayuhasena. The constitution was changed to make the country a constitutional monarchy, but not long after the army took control and adopted strongly nationalist policies.

During World War II Japan invaded Thailand and the government, under Field Marshal Phibul Songkhram, allied itself with Japan—not that it had much choice in the matter. However, the Thai ambassador in Washington refused to declare war on the U.S.A., and a number of prominent Thais were involved in the resistance to the Japanese initiatives, which stood the country in good stead with the U.S.A. in the postwar period.

After a brief period of democracy the army retook control of the government, putting Phibul in charge once more. In 1949 a *coup d'état* by the navy against him failed, but he was eventually ousted by his Defense Minister, General Sarit, in 1957.

Modern Times

Sarit died in 1963 and his successor, Field Marshal Thanom Kittikachorn, reinstituted limited parliamentary democracy in the late 1960s.

However, in 1971 military rule was restored. In October 1973, pro-democracy demonstrations by students were dealt with ruthlessly by the military government. The government's leaders appealed to the King to restore peace, and the Prime Minister and his Deputy were forced into exile.

The King appointed an interim prime minister who supervised the drafting of a new constitution. The following year democratic rule resumed, but the military felt that the apparent instability of the government boded ill for Thailand's survival at a time when three of its neighbors had fallen to Communism (South Vietnam, Laos, and Cambodia), and martial law was reimposed, this time with the King's backing.

More student demonstrations took place, with many of them joining the Communist insurgency movement that appeared to be gaining strength at the expense of the right-wing administration then in power. In 1977 the same military leaders who had put it in power replaced it with a more democratically minded government led by General Kriangsak Chompriand.

In the 1980s Prime Minister Prem Tinsulanonda presided over a period of relative stability, but his successors proved corrupt and unpopular, prompting another coup in 1991 by General Suchinda Kraprayoon. In 1992 General Suchinda appointed himself prime minister, causing student protests. Confrontations between the army and students led to a bloody massacre, and the King intervened to mediate a compromise between the opposing groups.

Thailand's economy had prospered in the 1980s and early 1990s, and the country was regarded as one of the "tiger" economies of Asia. Then in the middle of 1997 came an economic crash; currency speculation was rife, banks and businesses were bankrupted, construction projects were abandoned, and the Thai currency fell. Other economies of the region shared a similar fate. The readjustment has been painful, but the country is staging a successful recovery.

Thailand must surely be a contender for the world record as regards the number of *coups d'état* that have taken place in the twentieth century—some bloodless, others exceptionally bloody. However, there are positive signs that those turbulent days are over and that the country's evolving democratic structures are now more soundly based.

Since 1992 there have been no more coups, and the new constitution of 1997, designed to reduce political corruption, seems to be working well. In the elections to the Senate in 2000, a number of electoral contests had to be rerun because of allegations of electoral fraud. A similar situation occurred in the elections to the House of Representatives in 2001.

GOVERNMENT AND POLITICS

Thailand is a constitutional monarchy with a parliament consisting of a 200-member Senate (*Woothi Sapha*) and a 500-member House of Representatives (*Sappha Poothaen Rassadorn*). There is universal suffrage, and everyone over the age of seventeen is entitled to vote. Elections are held every four years, but until now no government has lasted the full term.

Candidates for the House of Representatives have to be at least twenty-five years old and hold a bachelor's degree. Four hundred representatives are elected on a constituency basis, and the remaining one hundred from party lists. The prime minister has to be elected by a majority in the House of Representatives. To become a minister one must be thirty-five or over. Candidates for the Senate must be at least forty and hold a bachelor's degree.

The Thai Party System

Normally a party is a loose alliance of individuals clustered around a key figure, not a grouping with a particular ideological persuasion. Party loyalties tend to be fickle, with party members ready to change allegiances at the drop of a hat. All elected governments have been coalitions and the latest one (2003) is no exception. Coalition governments tend to be unstable, which is one reason why no government until now has lasted its full four-year term.

The dominant party of the current coalition government is the recently founded *Thai Rak Thai* (Thais love Thais) Party, led by the millionaire businessman Thaksin Shinawatra, which has absorbed two of the smaller parties. Its junior partner is the longer established *Chart Thai* (Thai Nation) Party. The Democrats (*Prachatipat*) are currently the second-largest party and form the Opposition. The National Development (*Chart Pattana*) Party is the other significant party in the National Assembly (*Ratha Sapha*).

TOWN AND COUNTRY

The modern aspect of Bangkok—with its high-rise buildings, its well-stocked shops selling Western goods, its populace dressed in the latest fashions, its polluted air, and infernal traffic jams—may well suggest that this is a city like any other. The international beach resorts may not seem very different from those you find in other countries. But do not be taken in by appearances. Enter one of the many temple compounds around the city, leave the main thoroughfare and go down a back street, or take a long-tailed boat along a canal into the country, and you will discover a different Thailand that seems completely at variance with the hustle and bustle of the city. This is the real Thailand, where tradition is deep-rooted.

Bangkok dominates the country economically, culturally, and politically. Any provincial with ambition aspires to a job there, even though living conditions tend to be much more pleasant elsewhere. Much of industry and all the major companies are based or headquartered there; it accounts for more than half of the national total of telephones and cars—and this is why the city's traffic jams are so notorious.

Bangkok is the original name for the area, and means "The Village of Wild Plums." When it became the capital it was given a new name, *Krung Thep.* This is a shortened version of the official title for the city which is "The City of Celestial Beings, the Great City, the Residence of the Emerald Buddha, the Impregnable City of Indra, the Grand Capital of the World Endowed with Nine Precious Gems, the Happy City Abounding in Enormous Royal Palaces that Resemble the Heavenly Abode where the Reincarnated Gods Reside, a City Given by Indra and Built by Vishnukarm."

Several of Thailand's most historical monuments are situated here—notably the Grand Palace and the Temple of the Emerald Buddha, Wat Phra Khao. Bangkok, with its intricate network of canals, was once described as the "Venice of the Orient." Like Venice it is sinking, but unlike Venice several of the canals have been paved over to make roads. Modern Bangkok is polluted, dirty, and overdeveloped—and its infrastructure is creaking.

Attempts have been made to move the capital away from Bangkok, but have repeatedly failed, for despite the deteriorating living conditions, nobody is willing to leave. However, at long last brave attempts are being made to overcome the city's chronic traffic problems. In 1999 an overhead mass transit railway opened, known as the "Skytrain"; and forty years after the idea was first mooted, an underground railway system is being constructed. The first trains are scheduled to start running in late 2004.

The provinces are very different. No provincial city comes anywhere near Bangkok in size. The largest provincial capital is Nakhon Ratchasima, with around 430,000 residents, while Chiang Mai has only a quarter of a million. But 80 percent of the population lives in the countryside, cultivating the fields as it has over the centuries, though large numbers of country people drift to Bangkok to do seasonal work.

There is a strong sense of community in these places and unless they are on the tourist trail they are less affected by foreign influences. However, it is encouraging to see how the rural communities (including hill tribe communities) are beginning to share in the country's newfound prosperity.

Some Key Dates

11th C	Siamese (Thai) people settle in the valley of the Chao Phraya River in Khmer Empire.
c. 1240	Foundation of Sukothai as independent Thai kingdom.
1275–98	Reign of King Ramkhamhaeng.
1296	Establishment of the Lanna kingdom at Chiang Mai.
1350	Foundation of the Kingdom of Ayuthaya.
1432	Ayuthaya takes the Khmer city of Angkor.
1548	First of the Burmese raids.
1516	Ayuthaya signs a treaty with Portugal.
1558	Burmese conquer Lanna.
1598	King Naresuan of Ayuthaya expels Burmese from Lanna.
17th C	Foreign trade under royal monopoly developed with Chinese, Japanese, and Europeans.
1604	Dutch build a trading station in Ayuthaya.
1612	British open trading station in Ayuthaya.
1615	Burmese reestablish control over Lanna.
1656	King Narai ascends the throne.
1662	First French Catholic missionary arrives.
1684	First French embassy arrives in Ayuthaya.
1688	Death of King Narai. Siam expels European military advisers and missionaries, adopts policy of isolation.
1767	Ayuthaya is sacked by the Burmese. Taksin leads resistance and relocates capital of Siam to Thonburi.
1782	King Taksin goes mad and is replaced by King Rama I who relocates capital to Bangkok.
1821	British East India Company sends envoy to open up trading relations.
1824–51	King Rama III reopens Siam to European diplomats and missionaries.
1827	Lao king invades Siam, but is defeated.
1851–68	Reign of King Mongkut. European advisers help modernize government, legal system, and army.
1855	Bowring Treaty gives British merchants access to the Siamese market.
1856	Royal monopoly in foreign trade ended.
1868–1910	Reign of King Chulalongkorn. Siam modernizes further and develops railway network using Chinese labor. Becomes a major exporter of rice.

1893	Siam cedes Laos to France.
1909	Siam cedes four Malay states to Britain.
1932	End of the absolute monarchy. Bloodless coup forces King Rama VII to grant a constitution with mixed civilian-military government.
1935	Abdication of Rama VII. His nephew Ananda succeeds.
1938	Field Marshal Phibul Songkhram is prime minister.
1939	The country's name is changed from Siam to Thailand.
1941	Japanese invade. Thailand is forced to become an ally.
1945	Japanese withdraw. Thailand compelled to return territory taken from Laos, Cambodia, and Malaya.
1946	King Ananda dies. His brother Bhumibol succeeds.
1947	Phibul regains power in military coup, reducing the monarch to a figurehead.
1950	Enthronement of King Bhumibol.
1955	Political parties and free speech introduced.
1957	General Sarit Thanarat gains power in a bloodless coup. Military dictatorship.
1963	Death of Sarit. General Thanom Kittikachorn becomes prime minister.
1967–74	Thailand supports U.S.A. in Vietnam War.
1968	New democratic constitution promulgated.
1971	The constitution is annulled.
1973	After student demonstrations the military government is forced to resign.
1975	Cambodia, Laos, and Vietnam fall to the Communists.
1976	Student demonstrations are put down by army. Martial law is declared.
1977	The Government is ousted by military Revolutionary Council in a bloodless coup.
1980	General Prem Tinsulanonda forms coalition and country stabilizes and prospers.
1991	General Suchinda Kraprayoon takes over in bloodless coup. A civilian cabinet is formed.
1992	General election produces five-party coalition; General Suchinda Kraprayoon names himself prime minister. Violent demonstrations lead to a state of emergency. King intervenes and General Suchinda bows out.
1997	Thai economy crashes. New constitution drawn up.
2000	Millionaire businessman Thaksin Shinawatra becomes prime minister.

chapter two

VALUES & ATTITUDES

KNOWING ONE'S PLACE

Few social systems can have been as thoroughly worked out as that of King Trailok of Ayuthaya in the fifteenth century, who ranked the citizenry by a system of numbers (*sakdi na*). A slave was allocated five points, a peasant twenty-five, a craftsman in government service fifty, and so on. If you became a top official your score jumped to ten thousand.

The *sakdi na* system gave the right to certain grants of land commensurate with rank, and permeated all economic, legal, and social life for four hundred years or so. It was not abolished until King Chulalongkorn came to the throne in the late nineteenth century, and it would seem vestiges of the system live on in the Thai psyche.

Although there is more social mobility in Thailand now, there are many who accept their position in life unquestioningly. They reason that if you have low status in this life it must be a result of misdeeds committed in a previous life. In Buddhist belief the moral law of *karma* determines that if you lead a virtuous life now, the chances are that you will enjoy a better status when you are reborn. It is no use complaining, since everyone else is in the same boat. However, education is increasingly seen as the pathway to a good job, and this has led to a record 22 percent of Thais enrolling in higher education.

STATUS AND FACE

Many Thais aspire to positions in the civil service, even though most government jobs are badly paid. However, being a civil servant gives you prestige and security, however lowly your position. If you are a teacher (*ajarn*) you are especially highly regarded, though still poorly paid. Working in business, even if you are a very successful businessperson, is less well thought of. Wealthy people, however, are universally admired.

Work in an office or shop is more highly regarded than a manual job. At one time office girls would have long fingernails to indicate that they did not perform menial tasks. A pale complexion is also indicative of high status, and many Thai women go to great lengths to shield themselves from the sun. Medically, this is a more sensible idea than exposing oneself to the risk of sunburn and skin cancer through sunbathing, as many foreign tourists do.

It's Not the Money!

I once got talking to a seller of pornographic magazines in Chinatown, Bangkok. He was doing a roaring trade, and obviously earning good money, but confessed that he was dissatisfied with what he did for a living. His was a low-status job, and he wished he could get into a profession with status.

The people like the status that goes with a job, even if it is a non-job. In the Thai civil service, you will occasionally find people whose jobs have become redundant, but who still retain their splendid offices. To dismiss them would cause them humiliation or loss of "face"—a very important aspect of status. The Thais will experience shame if they do something that others would regard as dishonorable, and they expect to be treated honorably and not have their dignity offended.

Status is shown by the clothes you wear and the cars you drive, which is perhaps why in the boom years of the 1990s Thailand was one of the biggest markets for Mercedes Benz cars. Many Thais prefer to drive to work through horrendous traffic jams rather than travel by the new Skytrain, for the simple reason that they would lose face by so doing.

RESPECT FOR OTHERS, AND THE *WAI*

The Thais are respectful people. Children are brought up to respect their elders and to defer to authority. If a person has a higher rank than you in society, he or she is worthy of respect, and a good employee acknowledges the superiority of his boss and does not contradict him. Students respect their teachers and would not dare to argue with them or even ask them questions.

One of the ways the Thais demonstrate respect is to press their palms gracefully together, fingers pointing upward as if in prayer, and incline the head forward in salutation. This is known as the *wai*. It is normal for people to *wai* when they see a superior, and the recipient of the *wai* will *wai* back. The greater the difference in rank, the lower the head is inclined and the higher the *wai* should be. The inferior should always initiate the *wai*.

Educated and younger Thais who are used to Western ways are more likely to shake hands with a foreigner and do not expect foreigners to observe the custom of *waiing*. Nevertheless, if someone *wais* to you it is much appreciated if you *wai* back at them. But it is advisable to learn how to *wai* correctly to avoid committing any *faux pas*.

SELF-CONFIDENCE

Thailand has never been under foreign rule, so the Thais can hold their heads high and regard people from other nations as their equals. They come across as self-confident, and proud of their country, but never arrogant. They learn from an early age that Thailand is "Buddha's own country." They have savored independence for centuries and have much to be thankful for.

This self-confidence is reflected in their smart appearance. Cleanliness is important, and Thais think nothing of having several showers a day. They make a point of being well dressed, with clothes always spotless and neatly pressed. The Thai word for dirty, *sokaprok*, expresses disgust. Urban women, in particular, take a pride in their appearance, wearing smart clothes and making extensive use of cosmetics. They also smile a lot—simply because a smile always looks more attractive than a frown.

It is important not to prick the bubble of self-respect when dealing with Thais. They may criticize their government for its failings, but it is quite another thing for a foreigner to do so. They are sensitive to criticism, and if you start finding fault with any of their institutions they might feel you are criticizing them personally. If you criticize their monarchy or their religion you will be very unpopular.

SELF-CONTROL

In most situations the Thais exercise remarkable self-control. Even if they are experiencing personal problems they attempt to put a brave face on things, and betray little emotion. Anna Leonowens in *The King and I* whistled a happy tune when she felt low; but in a similar situation a Thai would just smile and maintain a calm dignity.

This does not signify that the Thais are bereft of feelings, and that they do not experience the same frustrations as you do when stuck in a Bangkok traffic jam. It is just regarded as bad form to express one's feelings overtly, to display anger or cause any kind of unpleasantness.

Furthermore, to behave in such a manner would incur the wrath of the spirit world (see Chapter 3, Religion and Tradition) and lead to loss of face. For the smooth running of society it is essential to keep one's cool. The Thais have a word for this: *jai yen*, or "cool heart."

This manifests itself in several ways. The Thais don't wave their hands about, or keep them in their pockets, which is considered bad manners. They also speak quietly—it is regarded as rude to raise one's voice. They rarely touch one another or embrace in public, and stand at a respectful distance from each other when talking. However, it is quite acceptable for people of the same sex to hold hands in public, with no sexual overtones.

Times are changing. Some members of the younger generation are starting to adopt Western manners, particularly those who have studied abroad. Young couples link arms and kiss and cuddle in public, much to the consternation of their elders. Yet one senses that as these young people approach middle age they will revert to tradition and regain their *jai yen*.

At times the bottled-up emotion reaches the breaking point and something has to give. This can result in violent acts, such as shouting abuse, damaging property, maiming, or even killing. For this reason, you should always be circumspect in your dealings with Thais and avoid acts that might be regarded as provocative. The Thais have long memories, and do not forget insults or provocation easily.

MAINTAINING SOCIAL HARMONY

In order to maintain some semblance of social cohesion the Thais try to keep their cool and avoid arguments. In a close-knit society it is regarded as bad form to cause dissension. One should endeavor to live harmoniously with one's neighbors and follow the Buddhist middle path that urges followers to avoid extremes. Getting angry or telling people off is unlikely to solve anything—in Thailand anyway. Anger is disruptive and they regard people who go around making a fuss and picking quarrels as hotheaded—or, to translate literally from Thai, "hothearted" (*jai ron*). The best advice is "keep your cool" and smile benignly, however frustrated or annoyed you feel.

The idea of maintaining social harmony has its roots in rural communities where people need to cooperate in order to survive. You work together in the rice fields, you harvest the rice together, and you meet together for traditional celebrations. Everybody knows each other's business, and the last thing you want is bad feeling between people.

One way of strengthening links is by doing people favors. The Thais have a do-as-you-would-be-done-by philosophy, reasoning that if you do someone a good turn he or she will feel grateful and will reciprocate the favor one day. If you are kind to someone, they will be kind to you. Thus you have a network of people who are mutually obliged to one another. The Thais call this concept *bunkhun*—indebted goodness. The *bunkhun* system often manifests itself as an indirectness in communication that makes it difficult for a foreigner to know what message a Thai is really trying to convey.

Sometimes the Thais are obliging to a fault. They put themselves to a great deal of trouble in order to comply with other people's wishes—an attribute which the Thais term *krengjai*. This manifests itself in various ways, for instance in being overconsiderate. For example, the Thai sees someone working, and may decide not to disturb him even if he has an important message for him. Or he may be inhibited about expressing his own opinions for fear they might disrupt social harmony.

He is in effect repressing his intentions or desires for the sake of the general good. When asking a Thai to do you a favor, it is important to check first that he will not be inconveniencing himself for you. Some will go far beyond the bounds of duty just to be obliging, perhaps missing an important appointment to run a trivial errand for someone else.

LOVE OF FUN

Although it may seem that the Thais must lead very stressful lives in their quest to maintain social harmony, they find an outlet for their pent-up energies by enjoying themselves. Thais like to have fun; they like parties, gossip, going to the movies, taking trips, and eating out together.

Wherever you go in Thailand you will hear the word *sanuk* being used—the Thai word for fun. Is Bangkok *sanuk*? Was a certain film *sanuk*? Was a party you attended *sanuk*? Even occasions like funerals, which Westerners regard as serious affairs, ought to be fun in Thai eyes. And so is work. The Thais do not draw a sharp distinction between work and pleasure in the same way as Westerners do.

The Thais are an exceptionally gregarious race when it comes to fun. They like to have a good time together and cannot envisage enjoying life in any solitary way. Their idea of fun tends to be unsophisticated and playful—usually with noisy music and bustling crowds.

Forget about the Protestant work ethic. Most Thais are easy-going people who refuse to work themselves to a standstill. Work is a means to earning a living, not the be-all and end-all of life, and has its roots in Thai village society. "All work and no play makes Jack a dull boy" more or less sums up this philosophy. Indeed the Thai word *ngan,* which means "work," also means "party."

So does that mean that the Thais have a lackadaisical attitude to work? Not really. Most of them work well and efficiently, and manufactured products from Thailand are of excellent quality. But work has to have a social dimension too, and if the fun element is missing people will see little point in giving of their best. People who put all their effort into their work and neglect their social life are regarded as distinctly odd. Perhaps Westerners who complain of increasing pressures of work could learn from this Thai attitude.

One of the nicest characteristics of the Thais is their tolerant attitude. If you make a terrible mistake, provided you are apologetic about it, people will endeavor to put you at ease by smiling politely and uttering the words *"mai pen rai,"* which means "don't worry" or "it doesn't matter." Why get upset about something? Nobody is perfect and besides tomorrow is another day.

However, outsiders can find the *mai pen rai* attitude extremely irritating. If a Thai driver backs his car into yours, you may feel that the damage to your car does matter. When he smilingly shrugs his shoulders, remember this is designed to defuse a potentially explosive situation, not to irritate.

GENEROSITY

The Thais are a generous people. If they have money in their pocket, they like to spend it, and they often spend more than they can really afford. They cannot understand people who put away cash for a rainy day, or who invite them out for a meal and expect them to split the bill. Such people are regarded as *kee niaw* or *ngok* —which are both untranslatable pejorative terms.

One can sometimes view such generosity as a manifestation of *bunkhun*—a way of making the recipients of your favor feel indebted to you and willing to reciprocate. But in many cases there is no such ulterior motive. A person who has a good heart (*jai dee*) is always cherished and respected.

THE IMPORTANCE OF THE HEAD

The top of the head is the most important part of one's body for a Thai because it is here that a person's spirit (*kwan*) resides. For this reason one should never touch a person's head, even if you are close friends, though between people in love this taboo is often broken.

If you do happen to touch a person's head accidentally a prompt apology is in order. Hairdressers are always most apologetic before they begin to deploy their skills on a customer. Patting the heads of small children is, however, accepted practice. Clothing associated with the head should also be treated with respect—try not to sit or tread on someone's hat, for example.

One way to demonstrate humility is to ensure that your head is kept lower than that of your superior. Thai kings used to sit on a high throne so that their subjects' heads were below the level of the royal feet; indeed one of the titles for the king is *Somdech Phra Chao Yoo Hua*—"The royal feet of the divine one above my head."

For a similar reason monks sit on a dais when the faithful come to visit; servants shuffle around the room in a stooped position if their employer is seated; and waiters and waitresses stoop when serving people in a restaurant.

If the head is the most important part of the body, the feet are the least important, and should be kept out of sight wherever possible. Never point at anything with a foot, or rest your feet on the table. This is regarded as the height of rudeness. Only in Thai boxing are feet allowed to touch the opponent's head.

ATTITUDES TO SEX
The Thais do not have any inhibitions about sex; they regard it as fun. Polygamy was long a feature of the Siamese court and prominent officials and nobles would show off their status by taking mistresses or minor wives (*mia noi*) in addition to having an official wife (*mia luang*) who would tolerate her husband's extramarital activities. The less well off had to be content with consorting with prostitutes. Old traditions die hard, and although the present monarch is monogamous, many leading politicians and businessmen have mistresses. It is reckoned that the majority of sexually active Thai men frequent brothels and massage parlors on a regular basis.

Yet there is a certain ambivalence about sex. Officially prostitution has been illegal in Thailand since 1960; establishments offering sexual services masquerade as bars, restaurants, and hotels, and the authorities are bribed to turn a blind eye to their true nature. The Thai language is redolent with double meanings, but one has to take care these do not intrude into polite conversation.

The Thais tend to keep their indiscretions private. They adopt the attitude that what you do in private is your own business; but one has to prevent improprieties from entering the public arena. Physical contact between the sexes in public places is frowned upon, but what goes on behind closed doors is fine.

Foreigners should not make the mistake of assuming that all Thai women are promiscuous. Most of them are not, and would be shocked if their charming demeanor were to be regarded as an invitation to have sex.

ATTITUDES TO FOREIGNERS

As we have already seen, the Thais have no postcolonial hang-ups about Westerners, simply because they were never colonized and regard Westerners as their equals.

The Thai word for European is *farang,* and you will hear the name used wherever you go in Thailand. Parents will point you out to their children, and often children will come up close to get a better look. Some may touch you for luck. *Farangs* are frequently a source of great amusement to the Thais, since they behave in such strange ways. The Thais watch the visitors intently, waiting for them to commit some *faux pas* or do something odd. However, in many of the international tourist spots foreigners are so numerous that they lose their curiosity value.

The Thais are particularly attracted to foreigners who behave politely and try to follow Thai practice. On one occasion I was sipping a beer with a friend at a roadside café in a holiday resort, when a Thai came up and greeted us. He said he wanted to meet us because we were dressed politely (*suparp*). On further investigation we found he was impressed because we were both wearing shirts and slacks in a place where everyone else was in T-shirts and shorts.

Thais are less impressed by foreigners who "go native" and dress as Thai peasants. On the whole, they prefer us as we are.

The Thais can be disarmingly direct, asking personal questions even when they hardly know you. They will ask where you come from, whether you are enjoying your stay, whether you are married and, if not, when you are planning to tie the knot. They may even ask how much you earn. You are not expected to answer properly or exhaustively, for this is merely friendly small talk.

The Thais admire people with pale skins, but you will find some who are afraid of people with dark skins, which they call "*kerk*." For this reason, darker-skinned foreigners have to work harder to earn their respect and friendship.

Are there any signs that the Thais' love affair with foreigners may be coming to an end? Mass tourism may benefit the economy, but it has its drawbacks. Some Thais feel they are being overwhelmed by the creation of international ghettoes along the coast; they also fear that the behavior of some foreign tourists and residents may have a detrimental influence on Thai youth. One can only hope that their traditional tolerance of foreigners does not turn into resentment.

chapter three

RELIGION &
TRADITION

Temples are dotted about the landscape of Thailand just as churches are in the West and mosques in the Middle East. Although the country's administration is secular, Buddhism is the dominant religion, and the King himself is a Buddhist. Buddhism is therefore an important influence on how the Thais behave and think, and has also inspired much of this country's greatest art. Even if you have no plans to visit temples you cannot but be aware of the all-pervading presence of Buddhism, and some understanding of it offers an insight into the Thai mentality.

THAI BUDDHISM: A BRIEF DESCRIPTION

What is Buddhism? The Buddha, meaning "enlightened one," was an Indian prince, Gautama Siddhartha (c. 563–483 BCE), who lived on the Indian–Nepalese border. After renouncing the trappings of his rank to become a hermit, he started to meditate on the suffering he saw about him and sought to discover the root causes. Eventually he attained the state of enlightenment (*nirvana*) under a banyan or *bo* tree, and in so doing escaped the cycle of rebirth and suffering that is the lot of mankind.

The Thai school of Theravada Buddhism differs from the Mahayana doctrine prevalent in China, Japan, and Korea. It harks back to the eighteen schools of ancient Buddhism known as Hinayana Buddhism (the Lesser Vehicle), which predate the emergence of the Mahayana doctrine (the Greater Vehicle) as a separate branch of the faith. More conservative and orthodox than the Mahayana school, Theravada Buddhism also has a large following in Cambodia, Laos, Burma (Myanmar), and Sri Lanka.

The early Buddhist influences came via the Dvaravati Mon Kingdoms established in southern Burma and west central Thailand between the sixth and ninth centuries CE. These were conquered in turn by Burma, the Khmer Empire, and the Thais.

Later Sri Lankan influences became dominant. The island had become a major center of the Theravada School in the tenth century, and by the thirteenth century missionary monks were active in the southern Thai kingdom of Nakhon Si Thammarat. From here it spread to Sukhothai, which became an important center for the faith.

Theravada Buddhists revere the historical Buddha and do not pay homage to the celestial Buddhas that Mahayana Buddhists worship.

The goal of Buddhism is to attain enlightenment, and to do this involves following the Noble Eightfold Path that the Lord Buddha revealed to his disciples.

- **Right View or Thought:** true knowledge and understanding; seeing the world as it really is.
- **Right Intention:** flowing from right thought, the intention to be in accord with reality resists evil, thinking with kindness and compassion.
- **Right Speech:** being aware of what you say; saying nothing to hurt others.
- **Right Conduct:** acting on right intention; abstention from harming living things, stealing, and improper sexual behavior.
- **Right Livelihood:** extending right view or action into daily life; earning a living in a right and just way that does not harm others.
- **Right Effort:** using what energy you have correctly.
- **Right Mindfulness:** being attentive to what is happening inside you and around you.
- **Right Concentration:** applying the mind in meditation and to the task in hand.

Buddhist Impact on Thai life

Although the goal of Buddhism is enlightenment, in practical terms Theravada Buddhists do not regard it as possible for laypeople to attain this state of perfection. The best a layperson can hope for is a reduction of suffering through the doing of good deeds and the avoidance of evil.

Performing good deeds enables you to gain merit, which Thais refer to as *tam boon*. This takes various forms: you present food, money, and gifts to the monks; you buy a caged bird and set it free; if you are wealthy you may even build a temple.

One way to gain merit is to enter the monkhood (*buat pra*). It is customary for around 50 percent of young Thai men to take this step for a minimum of three months during the Buddhist Lent. It is a rite of passage, so to speak, and may well take place when they return from studies abroad or before they get married. In this way they earn merit not only for themselves but also for their parents or benefactors. Others, including high-ranking figures, may also spend time in a monastery. One high-profile example is former Prime Minister Thanom Kittikachorn, when he returned from exile in 1976.

The avoidance of evil involves taking the Middle Way between an existence of extreme asceticism and one of sensual indulgence. A person's conduct should be governed by the five basic precepts of Buddhism.

To abstain from taking life.
To abstain from taking what is not given.
To abstain from sensuous misconduct.
To abstain from false speech.
To abstain from intoxicants that tend to cloud the mind.

In daily life some of these precepts tend to be more honored in the breach than in the observance. The Thais eat meat, tell lies, drink alcohol, and may also indulge in illicit sex. In this they are perhaps not so different from the adherents of other religions who, while paying lip service to the precepts of their religion, continually fail to live up to them.

Apart from offering moral guidance, Buddhism also plays an important social role. In villages and towns throughout Thailand the temple is the center of community life. Festivals and fairs take place on the temple grounds, and it is quite normal for the whole village to turn out for an ordination ceremony. At one time they were the only organizations offering schooling, secular as well as religious, to boys only, of course. In some areas this educational role continues.

Another Buddhist influence is the use of the Buddhist calendar in parallel with the Gregorian (Western) calendar. In Thailand this is 543 years in advance of the latter, so 2000 was the year 2543 BE (Buddhist Era.)

The Life of a Monk

During the morning you will often see a procession of monks dressed in their saffron robes walking along the streets with their begging bowls. People come out to offer them dishes of food, which have to be eaten before midday. For the rest of the day the monks fast.

A monk's attire consists of three pieces of saffron-colored cotton cloth. One is worn as a sarong; another is thrown over the shoulder; the third completely envelops the body.

Monks spend part of the day meditating or studying Buddhist scriptures. Many are also involved in the life of the community as teachers and advisers. They preside at funerals and other ceremonies. When a new business opens or there is a special event to be celebrated it is usual for monks to be present. The abbot of the monastery is responsible for everything that happens there, and is normally highly respected in the local community.

Nuns

It is possible for a woman to enter the temple as a nun, which involves shaving her head and donning a white robe—not the monks' saffron garment. Though she may take vows, she does not enjoy equal status with monks: in the *sala*, or assembly hall, she may not sit on the raised platform with them but has to remain with the laity. In common with laywomen they may not touch a monk or his robes or offer him anything directly.

A Temple Complex

A Buddhist temple does not consist of just one building, but of a number of edifices. These are the types of buildings you might come across, though not every temple will have all of them:

The *bot* is the most important building of the temple. Important ceremonies such as ordinations are held here, and the sanctuary is for the use of the monks only. It houses a Buddha statue and is surrounded by a ring of eight boundary markers.

The *viharn* is a hall where other ceremonies and meetings are held. The monks usually sit on a raised platform where they chant prayers and preach to the faithful, who kneel before them as they offer them food, garlands, and other necessities of life. Funerals take place here. The *sala ganprien* is a meeting hall.

A *chedi,* or *stupa,* is a monument, usually with a tapering spire, that houses relics of the Lord

Buddha or the ashes of royalty, monks, or prominent laypeople. It can be round, square, polygonal, large, or small. The largest is thought to be the bell-shaped *chedi* at Nakhon Pathom west of Bangkok—a landmark for miles around.

Every temple complex normally has a *bo* tree. The Lord Buddha attained enlightenment when sitting under a *bo* tree (which belongs to the fig family).

The monks' quarters normally consist of small houses, with a larger one for the abbot.

A temple library was traditionally situated in the middle of a pond to prevent the termites from getting to the books.

There may be a crematorium, a towerlike structure with steps leading to the place where the body is burned. Not all temples have one.

A *prang* is a Khmer-style temple tower adapted from Hindu architecture.

A bell or gong is used for summoning the monks to prayer.

Images of the Buddha

Buddha images should not be regarded as idols. Large or small, they are sacred, and should be treated with great respect. Some of them are huge and in a reclining position. You should avoid sitting on them or standing in front of them for a photo, as this would be regarded as sacrilege. Do not point at a Buddha with your foot, as this also would cause considerable offense.

VISITING TEMPLES

There is no objection to non-Buddhists visiting Thai temples, provided they exercise due respect. The normal advice is to dress modestly, which means no shorts and T-shirts. It is better for a woman to wear a skirt. You may get told off or refused entry to certain temples if you offend the dress code.

Some temples, especially in Bangkok, charge an entrance fee. When entering any temple building you should always take off your shoes. Most temples allow photographs, but it is always prudent to ask first.

Young monks, in particular, will be keen to practice their English on you. Do not expect to engage them in erudite discussions on theological matters, however, since these may well be novices, whose English does not stretch this far.

If you are visiting a monastery where foreign visitors are a rare occurrence, you may be invited to meet the abbot. If this happens, it should be regarded as an honor, and you should remember to lower your body so that the level of your head is below his, and *wai* respectfully.

Women and Monks

Women are not admitted to the monks' living quarters, though men can be. Women should not touch monks or their robes, nor should they hand gifts to them. If you wish to offer something to a monk either place it on the ground before him—he will usually spread out a white cloth for this purpose —or ask a man to hand it to him. Also, when traveling on buses, a women should never sit down next to a monk. Speaking to a monk, however, is permitted.

RELIGIOUS RITES

There are no set times for Buddhist worship, which centers around chanting, acts of devotion before a Buddha image, and offerings to a relic of the Buddha. When a number of people are assembled on a special occasion or on the Buddhist Sabbath (*Wan Pra*) the abbot or another senior monk may preach a short homily. *Wan Pra* occurs four times a month, on the days of the full moon and the other phases of the moon, and it is the day when monks are read the 227 rules for monks (*Pattimokkha*) and make confession.

There is no obligation to undertake a pilgrimage, as in Islam, but people do visit holy shrines in Thailand in order to gain merit. Some of these are on hilltops (such as Doi Suthep in Chiang Mai) and are reached by a lengthy flight of steps. On a hot day, climbing to the top is a strenuous activity, yet people of all ages and in varied states of physical fitness make the effort.

RELIGIOUS FESTIVALS

The dates of some festivals are determined by the lunar calendar, as Easter is in the West, so the actual dates vary from year to year.

Makha Buja occurs in February on the night of the full moon of the third lunar month and commemorates the occasion when the Buddha's disciples gathered spontaneously to hear him preach. There are candlelit processions around the temple and people give offerings to the monks.

Visakha Buja occurs on the night of the full moon of the sixth lunar month (May) and marks the Lord Buddha's birth, enlightenment, and death. Celebrations occur at temples.

Asanha Bucha commemorates the occasion when the Lord Buddha gave his first sermon at Benares and his founding of the Buddhist order of monks. It falls on the full moon of the eighth lunar month.

The day after is *Wan Khao Pansa.* This marks the start of the Buddhist Lent *(Pansa)*, when monks remain for three lunar months within the confines of the temple engaged in prayer and meditation. Many young men are ordained monks for this period, which coincides with the rainy season.

Wan Ok Pansa marks the end of the Buddhist

Lent. The monks are allowed to leave their monasteries and men who have been admitted temporarily resume their normal lives.

Tod Kathin is the time at the end of the rainy season that is celebrated with processions around temples and temple fairs. People visit temples in their home towns or villages and it is regarded as meritorious to help out a needy temple in a poor part of the country. Arriving at the temple, the faithful present the monks with new robes, pillows, food, and money. One of the great spectacles of the Kathin season was the Royal Barge Procession along the Chao Phraya River—only rarely performed these days.

THE BRAHMIN INFLUENCE

Brahminism—the forerunner of Hinduism—is another potent religious influence, especially in court ceremonial that follows the practices of the Khmer imperial court.

One of the major ceremonies of the Thai year is the Royal Plowing Ceremony, an ancient Brahmanic ritual that marks the start of the rice-growing season. This takes place at Sanam Luang, the park near the Grand Palace, on May 6, with the King presiding.

The river deities or spirits are honored in the delightful *Loi Kratong* ceremony that occurs on the night of the full moon in the eleventh lunar

month (usually November). This is a festival with
Brahmanic origins. Candlelit boats, traditionally
made of banana leaves folded to resemble a lotus,
are floated on rivers, canals, and ponds all over
the country. In this way Thais ask pardon for all
the wrongs they have inflicted on the spirits.

Brahmins are also astrologers, and are
consulted about propitious times to embark on a
new enterprise, such as marriage, the launch of a
new business, or the dedication of a new temple.

THE SPIRIT WORLD

Thai Buddhism as it is practiced is not
unadulterated Buddhism. It coexists with other,
earlier, animist beliefs such as a belief in
unpredictable and often malevolent supernatural
forces. These spirits have to be placated for fear
they may bring misfortune to one's household.

When Thais build a house, a hotel, or other edifice
they feel obliged to pay homage to the guardian spirit
of the land on which it is situated. They therefore
construct a special spirit house for it, often taking the
form of a miniature temple perched on the top of a
stand. People come to the shrine, kneel before it, and
light joss sticks and candles in honor of the spirit.

Many Thais also wear amulets in order to
ward off evil, which may have an image of the
Lord Buddha or of a monk.

OTHER RELIGIOUS GROUPS

Muslims
Most of the Muslims tend to be concentrated in the south of the country, bordering on Malaysia, but there is a sizeable community in Bangkok who have blended in with the Thai populace. On the whole they tend to be fairly strict in their observances.

Christians
Although there are a number of Christian educational institutions, especially in Bangkok, the number of Thai Christians is not large. Many local Christians are ethnic Chinese who reside in Bangkok, but missionaries have converted some of the hill tribes to Christianity. In Bangkok there are churches of all denominations catering to foreigners. Thais differentiate between Catholics (*krisadang*) and Protestants (*kristian*).

Animists
The belief that everything, whether animate or inanimate, possesses a soul or spirit is the earliest form of religion. As we have seen, certain animist practices and beliefs are present in everyday Thai life. Some of the hill tribes practise animism, though some have converted to Buddhism and Christianity.

chapter four

MONARCHY & MILITARY

Along with Buddhism, the monarchy, the military, and the civil service have played an important role in the affairs of Thailand. Visitors from countries with different traditions tend to overlook or misunderstand this phenomenon, partly because a Westerner's view of the Thai monarchy is bound to be colored by Yul Brynner's depiction of King Mongkut in the film *The King and I.*

The Rodgers and Hammerstein musical may be great entertainment, but it is a work of pure fiction. True, there was a King Mongkut who engaged Anna Leonowens as an English teacher for his children, but the idea that she danced around the palace with him or even initiated him into Western ways is far from the truth. The king in question was not an uncouth Oriental despot, but an enlightened ruler, as we shall see later. This chapter attempts to put matters into perspective.

THE MONARCHY TODAY

Thailand is still a monarchy, and the present King, Bhumibol Adulyadej, is a direct descendant of King Mongkut. He doesn't go dancing around the palace either, but he does play jazz. And while a casual visitor may not meet him face to face, it is impossible to be unaware of his existence.

A portrait of the King, often with the Queen and his children, graces every public building and the walls of many homes. The royal anthem is played in cinemas, on radio and TV, and on public occasions, and everyone stands to attention. The King's birthday and coronation, and the Queen's birthday, are celebrated as public holidays. The King's head appears on Thai banknotes, coins, and stamps. The King and other members of the royal family take an active part in ceremonial occasions. Newspapers, TV, and radio stations give prominence to his various activities.

The Thais are overwhelmingly royalist, and although currents of republican sentiment undoubtedly exist, republicanism has never really taken root in the country.

RESPECT FOR THE KING

The Thais have a tremendous respect for the King, as well as his consort, Queen Sirikit. King Bhumibol (known to the Thais as *rachagan tee gau* "the ninth reign") is the longest serving monarch in the world, having ascended the throne in 1946. Although in his portraits he looks stiff and a trifle severe—because of an eye injury sustained when he was a teenager—this outward appearance belies his true nature.

Governments come and go, military coups seem to have occurred with monotonous regularity during his reign, but the King survives unscathed and can be regarded as a stabilizing force in a region not noted for stability. He has also been a unifying force. Past governments have tended to regard ethnic minorities, such as the hill tribes of the north, as a nuisance and have made efforts to assimilate them even when they resist the idea. The King, by contrast, has gone out of his way to assist these ethnic minorities and other impoverished groups by setting up countless agricultural projects, some of which are designed to wean them away from opium cultivation.

King Bhumibol is above politics, and can only intervene when the nation's survival is at stake. "We could be crushed by both sides, but we are impartial," he explains. However, there have been times when he saw fit to intervene—in the riots of 1973, 1976, and 1992—and thankfully defused some very ugly situations.

Although now in his late seventies he remains amazingly active, and in the eyes of many Thais he has a status similar to that of the god-kings of the past. It is difficult to find any critical voice raised against him. Even the staunchest republicans—and there are not many of those in Thailand—admit that he does his job well.

Had he not become King, he might well have become a jazz musician: he is an excellent saxophone player and composes music, his most popular piece being *Falling Rain (Say fon.)* He also writes scholarly articles, poetry, and prose.

The Queen is similarly revered. You find no gossip in the Thai media on a par with the British newspapers' treatment of the British royals. Imported newspapers are censored if they have any scurrilous reports about the king and other members of the royal family.

THE CHAKRI DYNASTY

Everywhere you go in Thailand, especially Bangkok, you will find statues of Thai kings as well as roads named after them, so here is a short list. Note that the Thais usually refer to their kings not by name but by their reign, as in *rachagan tee nyng* (the first reign). The kings were renamed Rama by King Vajiravudh (Rama VI) after the hero of the Indian epic, the *Ramayana.*

Rama I, or Chao Phraya Chakri (1782–1809), established the Siamese capital at Bangkok on the opposite side of the Chao Phraya River to Thonburi and encouraged large numbers of Chinese to settle in the Kingdom. He expanded the country's borders to include parts of Laos, Cambodia, and the Malay Peninsula.

Rama II, or Phraya Buddha Lert Lah (1809–24), was less of a military strategist than his father. He was a poet, who wrote the *Ramakien*, the Thai version of the *Ramayana*. He was also a patron of the arts, including Thailand's greatest poet, Sunthorn Phu. Links with the West were reestablished during his reign after a gap of more than a hundred years: Portugal was allowed a consulate and John Crawfurd of the English East India Company concluded a commercial treaty with Bangkok toward the end of his reign. Rama II also sent two embassies to China.

Rama III (1824–51) continued Rama I's expansion plans and organized campaigns against Vietnamese incursions into Cambodia and other parts of the kingdom. The treaty he had negotiated with the British during his father's reign effectively staved off British incursions into the Kingdom. He warned his successor that future wars would be with the Western powers (notably the French and British), and that he should not trust them. Like his predecessors he was a patron of the arts and no mean poet.

Rama IV (1851–68) is the King Mongkut of
The King and I fame whose reign marked a
turning point in the fortunes of
Thailand. Faced with the
growing interest in the region
by the colonial powers he
encouraged diplomatic contacts
with the West and by skillful
negotiation managed to retain
Thailand's independence. His tolerance and open-
mindedness proved far more effective in dealing
with the British and the French than the
xenophobic and isolationist attitudes of other
rulers in that region.

As an abbot in the monkhood he instituted
wide-ranging reforms within Thai Buddhism, and
when he became king he modernized the
monarchy. He also saw to it that his sons received
a liberal, Western-style education. Employing
Anna Leonowens to teach them English was just
part of his grand design.

King Mongkut concluded treaties with Britain,
the United States, and other countries, opening
his country to Western commerce.

In 1861, during the American Civil War, King
Mongkut wrote to President Lincoln expressing
surprise that he did not use elephants in warfare.
He offered him a male and female elephant who
he felt could be allowed to multiply in the

American forests and later used in war and for lumbering. The President declined the offer on the grounds that the United States was too cold for them.

Rama V, King Chulalongkorn (1868–1910), is the most highly regarded of all the Thai monarchs, the present office-holder excepted. He was a great reformer who abolished slavery, established a modern administration along Western lines, and employed over five hundred foreign advisers. He reformed the judiciary and financial institutions, brought the railway and telecommunications to Thailand, established a department of public health, and set up a system of education.

He also founded a law school and civil service college that would later become Thammasat University and Chulalongkorn University. Under pressure from the colonial powers he was forced to cede four Malay states to Britain and western Cambodia and Laos to France, but largely managed to preserve his country's independence. October 23 is celebrated as Chulalongkorn Day and crowds gather before the equestrian statue of the king in the square in front of the old Parliament Building (originally the Throne Hall).

In addition to being an effective administrator King Chulalongkorn was a man of letters. He wrote a drama entitled *Ngo Pa*; a novel, *Nitra Chakrit*; a travel book, *Far from Home;* and a guidebook of ceremonies. He was a great patron of the arts and among the architectural achievements of his reign are the Marble Temple, the Ratbopit Temple, the Debsirindra Temple (in memory of his mother), and the Chakri Palace.

Rama VI, King Vajiravudh (1910–25), was the first Thai monarch to be educated overseas—at the Sandhurst military academy and Oxford in England. He founded the country's first university, Chulalongkorn University, in memory of his father, instituted compulsory education, and was a great patron of the arts. He passed laws to assimilate the Chinese immigrants and obliged Thais to adopt surnames. But he was also a lavish spender and dissipated some of the country's wealth. In World War I he was on the side of the Allies, and because of this Thailand became a member of the League of Nations and sent representatives to the Treaty of Versailles.

Rama VII, King Prajatipok (1925–35), was the last absolute monarch of Thailand. In a bid to reduce the large amount of debt incurred by his predecessor he made cuts to government services that made him unpopular. In 1932 there was a constitutional coup by a number of Thais who had been educated in

France together with young military officers, and he surrendered power immediately. In 1935 he abdicated in favor of Ananda, son of Prince Songkhla, and died in England in 1941.

Rama VIII, Ananda Mahidol (1935–46), was nine years old and at school in Switzerland when he became king, and made only a few visits to the country. In 1946 he was found dead of gunshot wounds in the Royal Palace. There is speculation as to whether this was an assassination, suicide, or an accident, but the truth is never likely to be known, and the subject is taboo.

WHO'S WHO IN THE THAI ROYAL FAMILY

H.M. Queen Sirikit is the King's much-respected consort. She used to undertake engagements all over Thailand, but has had to cut down on her activities of late because of poor health.

Princess Ubol Ratana (born 1951) is the King's eldest child. She raised a few eyebrows when she married an American whom she met while at university in the U.S.A. She is active in a charity she founded to counter drug addition. Her daughter, Ploi Pailin, an accomplished musician, appears in all the Thai celebrity magazines and is well liked. She has two other children.

Crown Prince Vajiralongkorn (born 1952) is the heir to the throne. He studied at school in

England and at a military college in Australia. He has two daughters and undertakes many official engagements.

Princess Maha Chakri Sirinthorn (born 1955) undertakes many duties on behalf the King and is much admired for her efforts to promote Thai values and traditions.

Princess Chulabhorn (born 1957) is the King's youngest child. A medical graduate, she travels widely promoting Thai science and research and supports a campaign to assist families with AIDS.

H.R.H. Princess Kalyani Wattana, the King's elder sister (often referred to as *Pra Phii Nong*) plays an active role in public life and is very supportive of the King.

ROYAL TITLES

It is possible that you will come across people with royal titles, especially in government, in diplomatic posts, and in academic life. Also, many Thais will refer to the people by their titles rather than their names. There are quite a few of them around. Here is a guide to who is who.

The King is called *Nai Luang* (which is the equivalent of His Majesty), and his more formal title is *Phra Baht Somdech Prachao Yu Hua* (The Royal Feet of the Divine One Above My Head). The Queen is *Phra Rachinee* (The Royal Queen) or *Phra Nang Chao* (The Exalted Queen Consort). The King's children are *Chao Faa* (Celestial Royal Highnesses); the Crown Prince is known as *Somdech Phra Borom*. The King's eldest and third daughters have the title *Chao Faa Ying*. The second daughter, the Princess Royal, has the title *Somdech Phra Thep*.

Phra Ong Chao (His Highness) means that the person is a grandson of the King by the male line, and *Phra Ong Chao Ying* is the granddaughter. They often put the initials POC before their names. The children of POCs (i.e. the monarch's great grandchildren) take the title *Mom Chao* (His Serene Highness) or *Mon Chao Ying* (Her Serene Highness) and the initials MC. In turn the children of MCs (the monarch's great-great grandchildren) take the title *Mom Rajawong* (Royal Personage), or MR. A *Mom Luang* (Minor Royal Personage) or ML is the child of a *Mom Rajawong* and the great-great-great grandchild of the King. The titles themselves are not inherited, but specific to the generation; the descendants of a *Mom Luang* bear no title.

When speaking Thai it is the practice to substitute a person's title for the pronouns "you," "he," and "she" (as in "Is Teacher going out?"). But all of these people are bound to speak excellent English, so you can avoid the pitfalls of protocol by speaking English.

THE ARMED SERVICES

The military has always been a major force in Thai politics. Some of the country's most eminent monarchs, such as Taksin and Rama I, were military men who led their troops into battle.

But since the 1932 revolution when the King was deprived of his absolute powers, the role of the military has been disproportionate. To Western eyes the idea of military rule is quite appalling. One cannot overlook the fact that the Thai military have at times been particularly high-handed—shooting cold-bloodedly at student protesters, for instance. But this kind of behavior has tended to be the exception rather than the rule and for much of the time the military's conduct has been relatively benign.

Some of Thailand's military leaders have worked very hard for the benefit of the country, restoring order out of chaos when military intervention was needed. In addition they have promoted economic development and helped to lay the foundations for the country's current prosperity.

Perhaps the leaders of the 1932 revolution were naive in assuming that a country that had only known absolute rule could change overnight from being an absolute monarchy to a democracy. In 1932 the country was undeveloped politically, with only a small, articulate middle class who had no real power base. With the power of the king removed, there was really only one functioning institution that could fill the void: the army. And this is what happened.

IMPORTANT MILITARY PRIME MINISTERS

Luang Phibul Songkhram (1938–57) is one of the most significant Thai political figures of the twentieth century, despite his many faults. Of humble origins, he worked himself up through the ranks of the army, eventually moving into politics. Under his influence Thailand became more nationalistic, militarist, and xenophobic. He disapproved of the Chinese domination of industry and fostered state enterprises—"a Thai economy for the Thai people." He also obliged the Thais—certainly those in Bangkok—to wear Western dress, feeling it to be more civilized. He allied himself with the Japanese and retook former Thai territories from the French. After the war he was forced to resign, but later returned as Prime Minister and gained American support for his tough anti-Communist stance. He was eventually deposed in a *coup d'état*.

General Sarit Thanarat (1957–63) is generally regarded as a strong man who reduced crime and uprooted corruption in the police. He instituted rural development schemes, especially in the northeast, and expanded the educational system.

He also encouraged the young King Bhumibol to take a more prominent part in the nation's affairs. A notorious womanizer, he boasted some one hundred minor wives, and after his death was found to have been a good deal more corrupt than the image he projected.

Field Marshal Thanom Kittikachorn (1963–73) was Sarit's Defense Minister and when he took over on Sarit's death he allied himself with the U.S.A. in the Vietnam War, allowing the Americans to have airbases for their bombing sorties over Vietnam and Laos. He restored parliamentary democracy in 1968, but reimposed military rule in 1971. During his period in charge American money caused the economy to boom, and this was accompanied by large-scale corruption among those in power. Demonstrations against his government and loss of army support forced his resignation and exile in 1973. He returned to enter a monastery in 1976, but this caused further demonstrations that led to more bloodshed and the reimposition of martial law.

General Prem Tinsulanonda (1980–88) is regarded as having been one of the best of all Thailand's prime ministers, and under his benign but strong influence Thailand enjoyed a period of growing prosperity.

General Suchinda Kraprayoon(1991–93) organized a bloodless *coup d'état* on the pretext that the civilian government was blatantly corrupt, and promising to clean up Thai politics. But when he eventually named himself Prime Minister, there was an outcry. His period of influence came to an end after demonstrations in 1993 and intervention by the King in which he publicly reprimanded the General and the Leader of the Opposition in a live television broadcast.

THE ARMED FORCES TODAY

In the old power order the king was at the top of the pyramid, ruling the kingdom with the assistance of three institutions: the civil service, commerce, and the army. Nobody else counted for much, so members of these three institutions were beholden to the king.

There has been a gradual change in attitudes since the abolition of the absolute monarchy, and the emergence of representative democracy. Nowadays these three institutions have had to learn to serve the people rather than the king— and the change has not always come easily.

One would like to think that Thailand has outgrown its need to have strong men controlling its affairs, that the days of military dictatorships are over, and that the nation has now become genuinely democratic. Thailand now possesses a sophisticated and growing intelligentsia with the organizational skills that once only the army and civil service possessed to any extent.

Although their role may appear to have diminished, army people are often found in important positions in government and commerce—on the boards of companies, for example. Serving army officers can no longer hold political appointments, so the link between the military and government is broken, but there are a number of former army officers now in civilian clothes in the cabinet.

It has been a long haul since the bloodless coup of 1932, but at last, after much trial and error, Thailand seems to be emerging as a genuine constitutional monarchy with solid democratic institutions.

The navy, although it is one of the largest in Asia, plays a less political role. Senior naval officers made a fatal misjudgment by launching a coup attempt in 1951 that went badly wrong. They kidnapped the Prime Minister, Phibul Songkhram, while he was performing a ceremony aboard the dredger *Manhattan*. But the army and air force stayed loyal to Phibul and when he was transferred to the navy's flagship, the *Sri Ayuthaya*, the air force bombed and sank it. The Prime Minister leaped into the river and swam to the safety of the bank.

chapter five

FAMILY & SOCIAL RELATIONSHIPS

Family life is of considerable importance to the Thais; it represents continuity and security in the face of a hostile world. Although differences can arise among the members of the family, every effort is made to keep these to a minimum so that the family system is not damaged. Unlike the West where nuclear families are the norm, in Thailand the extended family is more usual, and it is not uncommon for several generations of one family to live under the same roof. This happens particularly in the case of traditional Chinese families and aristocratic Thai families.

CHILDREN AND THE FAMILY HIERARCHY
As in Thai society, so within the family itself. A child quickly learns where he or she stands in relation to the other people under the same roof. Your elders are your betters in Thai tradition and should be given due deference. Mother and father are *mea* and *paw* respectively, and the child will learn to address them as *khun mea* and *khun paw*

(Mrs. Mother and Mr. Father). The child will be expected to show deference to elder siblings, too, and will call them *pee* rather than the normal word for "you." They will call him *nong* (younger sibling). When differentiation between the sexes is needed *pee chai* means elder brother, *pee sau* elder sister. *Nong chai* is younger brother and *nong sau* younger sister.

Whereas in the West we have relatively few nouns to describe our relations, the Thais have a proliferation. Grandmother is either *ya* (paternal grandmother) or *yai* (maternal grandmother); grandfather is *boo* (paternal grandfather) or *da* (maternal grandfather). Aunt will be *ba* (parent's elder sister) or *ah* (parent's younger sister). Uncle will be either *lung* (parent's older brother), *ah* (father's younger brother), or *nah* (mother's younger brother).

The Thais are very fond of children, and though they often pamper them they are strict in some matters. Children are brought up to know their place, to behave politely, and show respect— traits that carry over into adult life.

A minority of more cosmopolitan Thai families are now starting to question this apparent stress on subservience that could lead to excessive obedience and conformity. They feel the younger generation needs to be encouraged to express itself much more freely.

On the other hand, some members of the younger generation are following models that are not always ideal. They are seduced by Western influences, and, although there is so much well-designed clothing in Thailand, they demand imported designer fashion items and clothes.

NAMES AND NICKNAMES

To an outsider, Thai names seem inordinately long and complex. Most given names are of two or three syllables and the surnames are even longer. Past prime ministers have rejoiced in the ponderous names of Chatichai Choonhavan and Chavalit Yongchaiyudh. These names are derived from the Sanskrit of Indian culture, and the longer surnames are hardly ever used in speech.

Thais did not have surnames until 1913, when King Vajiravudh, wishing to make Thais conscious of family honor, passed a law compelling everyone to take a surname. Ethnic Chinese, who in most other countries have monosyllabic Chinese names, have adopted Thai names. Thais claim to be able to tell from a person's surname whether the person is ethnic Chinese or Thai, and influential or not.

Within the family and among friends it is unlikely that Chatichai and Chavalit will be addressed by these names. All Thais have nicknames that remain with them all their lives.

These are usually convenient one-syllable names and not always complimentary. Examples are: *Deng* (Red), *Uan* (Fatty), *Awt* (Tadpole), *Moo* (Piggy), *Noi* (Titch, or Little One).

FAMILY OBLIGATIONS AND NEPOTISM
A Thai has obligations to the rest of his family, however distant. If a second cousin comes down from the north to seek work in Bangkok, he will expect to be offered hospitality by his relations. If you hold an important position, your relations will expect you to find a job for them. This is all in the name of family solidarity. Nepotism may be frowned on in the West, but in Thailand it thrives.

Many Thais see advantages in the Thai system, for rather than appointing a perfect stranger you are offering a chance to someone whose strengths and weakness are well known to you.

BIRTH AND BIRTHDAYS
The birth of a child is not celebrated to such an extent as it is in the West. Some parents live in fear that the spirits (*pee*) will snatch the baby away; this superstition probably dates from the days of high infant mortality, which fortunately is not the case in Thailand today.

Problems start if people praise the child's good looks, for the spirits will be listening and are liable to snatch any pretty baby away from them. So when confronted with a baby, the Thais are more likely to comment on its ugliness than its beauty, and then the risk of kidnap by spirits is diminished.

The exact time of birth is normally recorded and given to an astrologer to predict the child's future and warn the parents of any steps needed to ensure a successful outcome. The American sociologist William S. Klausner and his wife were once asked if they could become the ceremonial parents of a baby girl, because an astrologer had predicted a bleak future for the child unless she was given to a foreign couple for adoption.

A Thai's life is reckoned in cycles of twelve years. The end of each cycle is a cause for special celebration (twelfth birthday, twenty-fourth birthday, etc.,) with the sixtieth birthday regarded as the most important of all. According to Oriental astrology each year is named after one of the twelve animals that came to bid the Lord Buddha farewell before he departed from the Earth—a rat, buffalo, tiger, rabbit, dragon, snake, horse, sheep, monkey, cock, dog, and pig. The animal ruling the year in which you were born is supposed to have a profound influence on your life and outlook.

MARRIAGE

Marriage is regarded as a desirable state since it provides for stability and the continuance of the race. The Thais always want to know if an individual is married or not.

Traditionally, courting couples are not supposed to be left alone, and if the boy takes the girl out, it is quite likely that one or more of her sisters will accompany them as a chaperone. It was also traditional for the groom to pay his parents-in-law a "bride price"—compensation to the parents for bringing up their daughter and a guarantee against desertion—but this is not so common nowadays.

Weddings are an important event in every Thai's life, and in order to ensure a propitious date and time it is usual to consult a Brahmin astrologer. He will give a very precise time, down to the nearest minute, for the wedding. This means that wedding ceremonies take place at odd times, such as 11:28 a.m. or 4:53 p.m.

On the morning of the wedding it is customary for the couple to go to the temple to give food to the monks and to visit the bride's and bridegroom's parents. Sometimes monks come to bless the house in which the couple will reside by sprinkling lustral water around. Another tradition is for an elderly couple whose married life has been exemplary to make the bridal bed and then lie down on it.

The wedding ceremony takes place at the chosen location, which could be the parental home or a hotel. The couple may be dressed in white or in traditional Thai costume. They kneel side by side in a crouching position, their heads joined by a white thread. Garlands are hung around their necks. They press their palms together and hold their hands over a silver vessel, and an elder pours lustral water over them from a conch shell.

The elder could be a senior member of the family, a high-ranking person who is a family friend, or their boss. For very high-profile weddings it could be the King or Prime Minister. The guests then line up in order of seniority and follow suit. There may be a speech, but it is normally brief.

It is the custom to give gifts, but knives, handkerchiefs, and the color black should be avoided. If the gift is a set of objects, such as glasses, odd numbers are preferred. Wedding gifts should be placed on a designated table. But do not be offended if your gift is not acknowledged. Thais are not effusive in their thanks, but this does not mean they are not appreciative.

At one time, as in other Asian cultures, arranged marriages were common, but this tradition appears to have died out, though you may still come across examples in rural areas.

DEATH

When a person is dying, a lighted candle is placed by their bedside. After death the deceased's family relatives wait until the candle has burned out before the body is washed and massaged. Then the eyes are closed, and in due course the immediate family sends candles, joss sticks, and flowers to extended family members before the body is put in the coffin.

The coffin is kept either at home or in the temple for a period that varies from seven to one hundred days. Monks chant extracts from the *Abhidhamma* scripture daily, and a longer service is held every seventh day. During this time well-wishers come to meditate and pay respects to the deceased and to the image of the Lord Buddha. They are offered refreshments, and may make a donation to the family to help defray costs. The women wear black dresses during mourning. The prolonged ritual is designed to create the illusion that the dead person remains with his loved ones, thus lessening their sense of loss.

The final stage is the chanting of the *Abhidhamma* followed by cremation of the body. You will see few tears at a Thai funeral, but rather a gentle stoicism.

THE POSITION OF WOMEN

As is the case elsewhere in Asia, women are socially inferior to men. Not that a casual visitor would notice, because far from seeming downtrodden many Thai women hold down important jobs—as company directors, hotel managers, civil service department heads, doctors, teachers, and lecturers. A number are highly educated and articulate, and many have traveled abroad, and exude an air of self-confidence.

Yet there is still a feeling that a woman's place is in the home. While the husband will go off to paint the town red with his friends, the wife stays at home. She often has control of the household finances, and many a Thai husband dutifully hands over his salary to his wife.

Some wealthier men have a separate home where they keep a concubine (*mia noi,* or "little wife"). This is regarded in some quarters as a status symbol, and they do not always limit themselves to one *mia noi.*

In country areas the subservience of women is more obvious. They serve their menfolk with food first and eat the leftovers later, and daughters-in-law are traditionally regarded as lazy good-for-nothings. It is not much fun for a young girl, especially if the marriage does not work out. Is it any wonder that so many flee their villages for the bright lights of Bangkok where they can earn a comparative fortune as bar girls, masseuses, or go-go dancers? All this sounds much more *sanuk* than being under the thumb of your mother-in-law. And who can blame them?

THAI HOUSES

The traditional Thai house is built of wood and is raised on stilts to protect it from floods. It consists of a large veranda, a number of rooms offering living and sleeping accommodation, and a thatched roof. In some places (for example, near Kanchanaburi) you encounter floating houses that were very much the norm in Bangkok until the reign of King Mongkut.

Modern Thai houses—in the towns at least—come in a variety of forms and tend to use brick and concrete rather than wood. However, many still have verandas on the first floor, which provide good ventilation. Mosquito coils are lit at night to deter these unwelcome visitors.

The more expensive houses will have air-conditioning units—in the bedrooms, at least—but others make do with fans. Ceiling fans are a particularly effective means of ventilating a room.

Most windows will have mosquito screens to avoid the need for a mosquito net.

Modern houses will have Western-style bathrooms with hot and cold running water. Others will just have a cold-water shower. Not that it matters, since in a hot climate showering in cold water is no ordeal. Where there is no shower appliance in the bathroom you will need to scoop water from a barrel into a container and throw it over your body.

In older houses and in the country the toilets tend to be of the "Oriental" type, which means you squat over them rather than sit on them. If they do not have a flush, you scoop water into a container and put it down the toilet.

You often see people in sarongs bathing in the rivers and canals. This practice is not to be recommended for visitors, since the water in such places is often badly polluted.

RELATIONSHIPS AT WORK

While the family circle is of utmost importance, there is a second circle of support that is important to a Thai: the workplace. Indeed, the best situation is if the place where you work bears a resemblance to your home, where you have colleagues you know and who will help you. It is an added bonus if some of them also happen to be members of your own family.

The ideal workplace should offer an individual a sense of security, with his department head or line manager playing the role of a father or mother figure. He or she needs to be someone you can trust and confide in, and who will offer you support where it is needed. In return the individual accepts the hierarchical structure and avoids speaking out of turn.

Once you are settled in your workplace, and it proves to be congenial, you will naturally choose to stay there as long as possible—ideally for life.

THAI RELATIONSHIPS WITH NON-THAIS

The Thais tend to look on foreigners either as equals or as an endless source of amusement. They regard the typical Westerner as a bit awkward and lacking in finesse, but they are prepared to overlook our shortcomings. After all, a foreigner can be a portent of good luck, and as you walk along the backstreets of Bangkok small children will run up and touch you for luck—or call out "Hey, you!" in order to demonstrate their English prowess.

However, there are cultural differences to be overcome. Foreigners tend to regard Thais as inscrutable because they do not express their feelings. The Thais have been brought up to be undemonstrative, and they are wary about forging instant friendships. They prefer to develop relationships over a period of time.

Love and the Foreigner

Problems may start when *farang* boy meets Thai girl. If they are seen out together the Thais tend to believe the worst—that the boy's intentions are far from honorable and that the girl is either a prostitute or his concubine. Even Thai women who are legitimately married to *farangs* can be the butt of unkind remarks. There does not seem to be a problem if the husband is Thai and the wife foreign. Indeed, single foreign women visiting Thailand are apt to receive proposals of marriage.

The uneasiness occasioned by "marrying out" persisted when the King's eldest daughter married an American in the 1970s. Though she was by no means the first member of the royal family to marry another national—a former potential heir to the throne married a Russian and was debarred from becoming king—Thais were uncomfortable with the match and preferred not to talk about it.

Nowadays, intermarriage is becoming more common and in some circles attitudes are becoming more relaxed. But for a Thai woman who is not married, there could still be a social stigma attached to going out alone with a foreigner. Going out in a group with non-Thais that includes other women, however, is much more acceptable.

VISITING PEOPLE AT HOME

Most Thais prefer to take people to a restaurant
rather than invite them to their homes for a party or
meal. One reason is that their homes may be small,
or crowded with relations. Well-to-do people who
have suitable, and often lavish premises, entertain at
home from time to time. If a Thai does invite you to
his home, however luxurious or humble, it is a sign
that he regards you as a true friend.

On entering the house you should take your
shoes off as a sign of respect. There will normally be
chairs, but if not you should sit on the floor on your
heels, not with your feet sticking out. Don't expect to
be shown around the house. Your host will have a
specially designated sitting room for receiving
visitors, and this is where you should remain.

It is a nice idea to take a small gift—
flowers, confectionery, or cookies are
perfect—attractively wrapped, if possible. Men
appreciate brandy or whiskey, unless they happen
to be Muslims. But they will not shower you with
thanks or even open it in your presence, as this
would detract from the worth of the gift.

chapter six

TIME OUT

EATING OUT—THAI STYLE

The Thais enjoy eating out, and everywhere you go in Thailand you will find excellent restaurants, more often than not run by Chinese. Although the rich may have dinner parties in their homes or gardens, it is more usual for a Thai to invite you to eat out in a restaurant. The subject of Thailand's excellent food is covered in Chapter 7, Food and Drink.

Eating out in Thailand is a very informal activity, and Thai guests will be relieved if you take them out to a Thai or Chinese meal rather than a formal, four-course Western-style dinner. It is normal to have a variety of dishes spread out before you from which you pick and choose. There is no need to stand on ceremony, and when the food arrives everyone digs in. Fork and spoon are the usual eating implements, though chopsticks are often used for noodles. In Chinese restaurants there is usually a succession of courses, with the arrival of the soup signaling that the end of the meal is nigh.

The idea of "going Dutch" when paying the bill is completely alien to Thais. If you invite a group of Thais out to lunch or dinner, you will be expected to pay for everybody. (*Kaw bin duai ne krab/ka* means "May I have the bill?") If a Thai invites you, he will foot the bill. One point of etiquette: if you wish to catch the attention of the waiter, beckon to him with your fingers pointed downward.

TIPPING

In Western-style hotels a service charge is normally added to the bill; in other places it is taken for granted that a tip is included in the price, but you may leave a small tip if you wish.

There is a huge range of restaurants in Thailand, offering Western, Thai, Chinese, Indian, Japanese, and other cuisines. A number offer entertainment as well as food. For men there is an unusual type of eating establishment, sometimes dubbed "human fork" restaurants, where hostesses feed and entertain their clients. These are popular with Thais, Chinese, and Japanese. Fast food restaurants and coffee shops are popular with younger Thais.

SHOPPING

Although Thais tend to believe (mistakenly) that
Hong Kong and Singapore are the shopping
meccas of southeast Asia, you can buy virtually
anything in Bangkok, often at bargain-basement
prices. Imports, notably foods, tend to be
expensive, so if you must eat cornflakes, cheese,
and pickles, expect to pay through the nose!

Thailand's industrial base has expanded
enormously in the past thirty years, and the
country now has a range of factories producing
electrical goods, textiles, pharmaceuticals, and so
on. If you want to go on a shopping spree you will
find most of these local products reasonably
priced and of good quality.

Some foreigners get annoyed because they feel
they are being charged more at markets than a Thai
would be, but vendors tend to price their goods
according to a person's ability to pay and they reason,
correctly, that a foreign tourist is well-heeled
compared with most of the Thai customers. If you feel
you are getting a raw deal, be prepared to bargain; this
is expected of you. If you can bargain in Thai, a vendor
will be so surprised and delighted that he (or, more
likely, she) will be more willing to give you a reduction.

Department stores, supermarkets, and hotel
boutiques tend to have fixed prices, which are
clearly marked. A number of foreign retailers have
branches in Thailand, but generally speaking the

smaller shops are much more fun. The Siam Square and Pratunam areas have a very wide range of shops, but you have good shopping facilities in most areas of Bangkok, including the major business area around Silom and Suriwong. There are several excellent markets, including the famous Floating Market, which is often the ultimate destination of city canal tours.

In the provinces you will also find a wide range of goods on sale, even in the smallest townships. Most of the large hotels and tourist centers have souvenir shops selling Thai handicrafts. Thai silk, bronzeware, lacquerware, Celadon pottery, and wood carvings are among the most attractive items.

Caveat Emptor

Buyer beware! Every year thousands of visitors are conned into buying *objets d'art* they believe to be genuine, but which are not. At archaeological sites like Ayuthaya, for instance, people will approach you offering to sell you genuine antiques that turn out to have been made last week and skillfully aged. A genuine antique is likely to be expensive, and if you plan to take it out of the country, you may well need to procure an export license.

You need to exercise particular care when buying jewelry, especially when approached in the street. Reputable dealers do not solicit in this way, nor do they organize special promotions. All claims as to the value of the object need to be verified carefully, and if you have any doubts as to the reliability of a jewelry dealer you should check with the Tourist Assistance Center of the Tourist Authority of Thailand. The Tourist Authority Web site is www.tat.or.th.

SIGHTSEEING

There are many regular guidebooks on Thailand, including excellent locally produced publications and Web sites, and an extensive section on travel would be superfluous here. However, it is worth mentioning just a few of the interesting sights in and near Bangkok, and in more distant locations.

In Bangkok

The oldest site is the Grand Palace complex, which includes the Temple of the Emerald Buddha (Wat Phra Keo). This was begun in 1782 by King Rama I and continued by his successors.

The National Museum, which houses a fine collection of antiquities, offers a fascinating introduction to Thai history and art, as do Thailand's other historical museums.

A boat trip on the Chao Phraya River is a must, enabling you to see Bangkok as it once was—a complex of floating houses and shops ranged along the river. You will also get spectacular views of Wat Arun (Temple of the Dawn) and the Grand Palace.

Close to Bangkok
Nakorn Pathom and Kanchanaburi
These can both be managed on a long day trip. The first boasts the largest Buddhist *chedi* (shrine) in Thailand, while the second is famous for the "Death Railway," built with forced labor during World War II by the Japanese, linking Thailand to Burma. There are war cemeteries to visit here, spectacular scenery, and a museum. You can get to both places by bus or train.

Ayuthaya and Bang Pa-in
Both are on the Chao Phraya River. The first is the former capital of Siam. The latter has a royal palace built by Chulalongkorn and a number of other buildings in European, Chinese, and Thai styles. There are train and bus services, but the nicest idea is to take a river trip from Bangkok.

Hua Hin and Petchburi
Hua Hin is Thailand's oldest seaside resort and, though extensively developed in recent years, is

regarded as far more relaxing than the popular resort of Pattaya. On the way a visit to Petchburi is possible. This is a small provincial city with a number of attractive temples. Both can be reached by bus or train.

Further away
Chiang Mai

This is the capital of the north and famous for its craftsmanship—textiles, wood carvings, pottery, umbrellas, etc. Among the sights worth seeing are the Doi Suthep temple and the Tribal Museum. This is a useful center for exploring other places in the north, such as Chiang Saen on the Mekhong River and Chiang Rai. You can travel to Chiang Mai by air, train, or bus.

Sukhothai

The former capital of Siam, close to the modern town, stretches over a wide area and has been designated the Ramkhamhaeng National Park, after the famous King of Sukhothai. Bus and train services operate to the city from Bangkok.

Nakorn Sri Thammarat

An important cultural center in the south of Thailand, once the capital of the Tambralinga kingdom. It boasts an excellent museum, the largest temple in the south, Wat Phra Mahathat, and Khao Luang National Park. There are air, train, and bus services to the city from Bangkok.

CULTURAL LIFE

Thailand has a rich culture that goes back many centuries. It can trace its origins to India; the eminent French scholar Georges Coedès included Thailand among the Indianized states of southeast Asia. However, the cultural influences, although emanating from the Subcontinent, entered the country via Burma, the Khmer Empire, and the southern kingdom of Srivijaya.

The Thais are proud of their cultural achievements, and with reason. But to appreciate Thai culture properly some background knowledge is helpful. The bookshop at Silpakorn Fine Arts University has an excellent range of literature on this subject, and if you would like to engage a guide or go on a guided tour the Tourist Authority of Thailand (TAT) can help. The following lines offer a brief introduction.

There are two important influences on Thai culture. One is Buddhism. The other is the *Ramayana*, the Hindu epic poem written in Sanskrit between 500 and 100 BCE by the sage Valmiki. The epic eventually spread to Indonesia,

Cambodia, Thailand, and Laos, and King Rama I wrote a version entitled the *Ramakien*. Themes from the epic are present in Thai murals and Thai classical dance.

Thai Dance

Thai classical dance (*lakhon*) was originally performed only at the royal court, but it can now be seen in theaters (notably the National Theater) and is often performed at wedding parties and other celebrations as well as in tourist restaurants.

The whole of the *Ramakien* would take days to perform, and a performance normally consists of just one episode. A chorus and narrators recite the narrative with musical accompaniment. The dancers tell the story through the use of stylized gestures and postures, and their movements are very slow. They hold their bodies straight from the neck to the hips and move them up and down with knees bent stretching to the rhythm of the music. Their brocaded costumes resemble the dress worn by royalty and mythological figures in old mural paintings. Masks are worn where a character is a demon or monkey.

Classical Music

Thai classical music uses a tonal system different from Western music, but those who are acquainted with Indonesian gamelan music will find many similarities. Unlike Western music which has full tones and semitones in the octave, Thai music has an eight-note octave consisting of full tones.

Among the instruments used are:

The *ranad* or Thai xylophone is usually slightly curved and resembles a boat.

Drums (*glong*) come in a variety of shapes and sizes; the shallow drum is known as the *ram mana*.

The *kawng* is a gong; one common variation is the *kawng wong yai*, which is a series of gongs (*kong*) suspended on a circular frame.

The *saw* is a stringed instrument that is played with a bow. Its body is made from half a coconut shell.

The *ching* are cymbals.

The bamboo pipe (*pee*) is a type of oboe.

The orchestra that accompanies Thai classical dance performances—known as a *pipat* orchestra—usually includes a *ranad, pee, ching, kawng wong yai,* and a *glong.*

Sculpture and Architecture

Just as Western art is categorized by various styles—such as Classical, Baroque, and Rococo—so is the art of Thailand. One can appreciate these styles by observing the various depictions of the Lord Buddha.

In the *Dvaravati* period (sixth to the twelfth centuries CE) the statues have a broad face and well-formed features. In the southern *Srivijaya* period (seventh to thirteenth centuries) the features are well proportioned and show more direct Indian influences. The *Lopburi* style is much more gentle and benign. Statues from the *Sukothai* period (thirteenth to fourteenth centuries) are notable for their graceful curves and oval faces. Art historians consider that this period represents Thai art at its most refined and spiritual. Buddha statues from the *U Thong* or *Early Ayuthaya* periods (fourteenth century) have squarish faces, thick lips, and smiling mouths. It is at this point that the Dvaravati, Khmer, and Sukhothai styles merge. During the *Ayuthaya* period (fifteenth to eighteenth centuries) there is a move away from the simplicity of the earlier styles and the figures become much more ornate. The *Rattanakosin* style (late eighteenth century onward) is the style associated with the Chakri dynasty.

Some people are puzzled by the appearance of Thai Buddha statues. They are based on the description of the Buddha as it appears in Pali texts, which now appears to be a mistranslation. Most statues, of whatever style, have the following characteristics: a protuberance on the top of the skull; spiral curls; distended earlobes; arms long enough to enable him to touch his knees without stooping; flat foot soles; and projecting heels.

Although the Buddha is normally represented in the sitting position, he is also depicted in standing, walking, and reclining postures; the latter shows the Buddha entering Nirvana. There are a number of different hand gestures which usually depict meditation, calling the earth to witness, teaching, and dispelling fear. In some cases the Buddha is seated on a lotus flower, in others on a *naga* serpent, a reminder of how the Hindu god of the underworld saved the Buddha from drowning as he was meditating.

Wat Benchamabopit in Bangkok, popularly known as the Marble Temple, has a cloister containing fifty-three bronze Buddha statues that display all periods of Buddhist art from Thailand and neighboring countries.

Much of the Thai architecture from the past is religious. Most temples have the steeply sloping roofs with green and saffron glazed tiles found in Khmer architecture, and have horn- or beak-shaped finials on the ridge ends. You often find statues of demons surrounding the temple, whose duty it is to guard against evil spirits. One is tempted to draw parallels with the gargoyles found on medieval churches.

POPULAR CULTURE

Popular Theater (*likay*)
Troupes of strolling players perform all over the
country, often at temple fairs. The actors
improvise the dialogue, lyrics, and plot of the play
making great use of puns and topical allusions.
Music is provided by a type of mouth organ (*ken*)
consisting of fourteen pieces of cane or bamboo.

Shadow Plays
Puppets with movable arms,
which originated in the south of
Thailand, or larger
immobile ones mounted
on sticks are manipulated
by puppeteers behind a backlit
screen. These are known as *nang
talung* and *nang yai*. A similar
tradition exists in Indonesia.

Cinema
Thailand has a thriving film industry that
produces films of varying quality. These
generally incorporate songs, humor, and
slapstick. Most of the films are for local
consumption, but one or two have recently made
it on to the international film circuit. Leading
film stars include brother and sister Willy and

Kateriya Mackintosh, who happen to be half Scottish, and whose films have a big following, particularly in the provinces. Chinese, Indian, and Western films are also popular.

Popular Music

The Thais have a large appetite for pop music, some of which sounds extremely schmaltzy. Nowadays there is a trend toward more Western-sounding pop music, of which one of the leading exponents is Thongchai Macintyre, known as Bird (who also seems to have Scottish blood pulsing in his veins). Other popular singers are Masa Wattapanich and Patiparn Pattavikan. Pongsit Kamphee is a leading exponent of folk rock.

Popular Dance

Thai folk dances have catchy rhythms and at celebrations it is quite usual for people to take to the dance floor and sway to the beat of the music, gesturing gracefully with their hands. The most popular dance is the *ramwong,* which was introduced by Phibul Songkhram to counteract the influence of Western ballroom dancing. Thais are very pleased if foreign visitors join in, however rudimentary their dancing skills. Folk dances (*rabam pun muang*) are associated with rice-planting and harvesting festivals as well as religious celebrations.

SPORT

Thai Boxing (*muay thai*)

This boxing looks a good deal more ferocious than the international variety, as the participants use their feet as well as their fists, although head butting is prohibited. It was once banned because of the damage boxers inflicted on each other, but regulations have since been introduced that govern the sport—the Thai equivalent to the Queensberry Rules. There are two major boxing stadiums in Bangkok—Lumpini and Rajdamnern. Boxing bouts also take place in the provinces.

Martial Arts (***krabi krabong***)

The Thais do not fight only with their feet; they use swords, staffs, clubs, and halberds, and you can see demonstrations of these skills in the various theme parks and restaurants. In a boy-girl fight, it is usually the girl who wins.

Fish Fighting

The Thais breed fish for these contests, and a pedigree champion has been known to attack for six hours. The loser is the fish that gives up the fight first. Cockfights are also held.

Bullfighting

This is a popular pastime in the extreme south of Thailand. But there are no matadors and no deaths—just two bulls pitted against one another.

Kite flying

This is a popular pastime in the hot season, as is kite fighting in which the male kite (*chula*) sets out to ensnare the female kite (*pukpao*).

Takraw

This game involves keeping a woven rattan ball in the air without using one's hands. A variation on this has rules similar to basketball.

Other more familiar sports are football (soccer), rugby football, horse racing, and golf. There are two racecourses in Bangkok—the Royal Turf Club and the Royal Bangkok Sports Club. There are excellent golf clubs available, which attract the better off Thais and many Japanese.

HOLIDAYS AND FESTIVALS

There are several festivals during the year, and foreigners are welcome to attend. Indeed, in the tourist resorts some festivals seem to be specially organized for the visitors. Unless otherwise stated, all of these are public holidays when banks, offices, and

FESTIVALS

January 1: New Year's Day

This could be regarded as the Thai equivalent of Christmas, when Thais send each other cards and give presents.

Late January–mid-February: Chinese New Year

The date depends on the New Moon. Not a public holiday as such, but many Chinese businesses close for celebration.

February:* Makha Buja Day (See Chapter 3.)

April 6: Chakri Day

This honors the present royal dynasty. (See Chapter 4.)

April 13–15: Songkhran

The traditional start to the Thai year, when it is the custom to bless one's elders by pouring lustral water over their heads. Unfortunately, this is a tradition that has changed for the worse over the years, and now in the provinces people regard it as great sport to throw buckets of water over one another.

April 14: Family Day

May 1: National Labor Day

May 5: Coronation (or Enthronement) Day

This commemorates the enthronement of King Bhumibol in 1950 and is usually marked by official celebrations.

May 6: Royal Plowing Ceremony Day (See Chapter 3.)

May:* Visakha Buja Day (See Chapter 3.)

July:* Asalha Buja Day (See Chapter 3.)

July:* Khao Pansa

The start of Buddhist Lent. In parts of the northeast Khao Pansa is celebrated with a Candle Festival.

August 12: H. M. The Queen's Birthday

October:* Tod Kathin (See Chapter 3.)

October 3: Chulalongkorn Day
Celebrations take place in honor of King Rama V.
(See Chapter 4.)

November:* Loi Krathong
Not a public holiday as such, but one of Thailand's nicest
festivals (see Chapter 3). People float little rafts on the rivers
and canals and sing in Thai the refrain: "Let us float our
krathongs together; When we do it, it brings us joy."
In Chiang Mai this festival is called Yi Peng.

November:* The Annual Elephant Roundup
This takes place in Surin Province, in the east.

December 5: H. M. The King's Birthday

December 10. Constitution Day

December 31: New Year's Eve

* date varies according to the lunar calendar

the civil service are closed. Most have fixed dates, but
the religious festivals follow the lunar calendar and
differ from year to year. In addition to the national
celebrations there are also plenty of local festivals.

NIGHTLIFE
Thai nightlife divides into the perfectly respectable
and the men-only brands. Many of the hotels have
nightclubs and bars that welcome both sexes and
offer musical entertainment and sometimes cabaret

with international stars. There are also plenty of excellent restaurants that serve Thai food and put on demonstrations of Thai dancing, music, and martial arts.

Bangkok has all the entertainment that you would expect to find in a cosmopolitan center, including classical and pop music concerts as well as plays performed by local and visiting groups. Seaside resorts have entertainment for foreign tourists ranging from cabaret to all-night disco parties on the beach. A glance at the Friday editions of the Bangkok English-language newspapers will give you some idea as to what is going on. Chiang Mai, Hua Hin, Pattaya, and Phuket have weekly English-language papers that give prominence to entertainment in the immediate vicinity.

THE SEX INDUSTRY

Thailand has also gained a certain notoriety for sleazier types of after-hours entertainment, with its many massage parlors (*ab ob nuat*), bars, and "tea-houses." While not all of these offer sex as part of the package, a large number do; the so-called "short-time" hotels, which often have bedrooms bedecked with mirrors on the walls and ceiling, offer little else.

Visiting a massage parlor can be an intriguing experience. A bevy of young masseuses in white coats sit behind a one-way glass screen wearing numbered badges. You pick your number, and the masseuse will usher you into a cubicle where she will strip you of your clothes, bathe you, and massage you. It is customary to give the masseuse a tip if you are pleased with the service.

There are bars all round Bangkok catering to foreigners, some with hostesses, others without. The biggest concentration of bars is in the area known as Patpong. Once a single short street (*Soi Patpong*), it is now a huge complex of bars offering entertainment to suit every taste, including go-go dancing, lap dancing, striptease, and plenty of noise. Bars in other parts of Bangkok, including *Soi Cowboy* (Cowboy Street!) off Sukhumwit Road, tend to be less raucous, more relaxing, and much cheaper.

In most of the bars there are hostesses who will help you to while the evening away with their limited English. Most are graceful and charming, but a minority seem to have learned their English and their manners out in the Wild West. Put it all down to foreign influence.

The girls earn their living by getting customers to buy them drinks, and every half hour (or more frequently) they will request another drink—politely, of course (Thais never hustle!). Some will offer further favors after hours. Should you want to take one of them out before the bar closes, you may have to pay the bar a fee to release them.

A number of the short-time hotels catering to after-hours activities have parking spaces directly under the bedrooms. You park your car and curtains are drawn to conceal the model and its license plate from prying eyes and protect its owner's anonymity. Sex is tolerated in Thailand, provided it is discreet.

Moralists are sometimes shocked at the number of Thai girls working in massage parlors, bars, and similar institutions. A survey by Chulalongkorn University estimates that there are 200,000 commercial sex workers in Thailand. However, before one blames Western sex tourism solely, one should bear in mind that the majority of their clientele are Thais and local Chinese men.

The job holds many attractions for the girls: it pays better than most other jobs (and Thai women often have a pragmatic outlook); the working conditions are better (air-conditioning, the company of their workmates); and it is far more enjoyable (*sanuk*) than working in a factory or planting rice. And since they are often far from home, who is to know what they are up to?

A fair proportion are country girls who hope to make their fortune and return to their villages one day with money jingling in their purses. After a few years a large proportion return home, reintegrate into the life of their community, lead respectable lives, and possibly get married. Some may be the chief breadwinners for their families back home.

TWO WARNINGS

Prostitution

Thailand's reputation for sex tourism has brought health and social problems. To combat AIDS and child prostitution the authorities have started to clamp down, and prostitution is, in fact, illegal. Those living on immoral earnings face heavy penalties. Visitors caught having sex with anyone under the age of eighteen could land in prison.

If you must have sex, for your own protection use a condom. The Thai word for this is *meechai*, named after the well-known figure Dr. Meechai Viravaidya, who instituted Thailand's highly successful family-planning campaign.

Drugs

The Thai government is anxious to eliminate the drug culture that is now affecting some younger Thais, and they seem determined to succeed. In early 2003 the police hunted down hundreds of drug dealers, many of whom were killed in the operation. Foreigners are not above the law, and in recent years numerous Europeans caught possessing or smuggling drugs have been prosecuted. Those who are convicted languish in Thai jails for lengthy periods.

chapter seven

FOOD & DRINK

Thai cuisine has an excellent reputation outside the confines of the country, and many towns in Britain, Australia, and North America can boast at least one restaurant specializing in Thai food.

However, the Thai food you eat at home has often been modified to suit Western taste buds, and in Thailand itself you may find it far spicier than you ever imagined food could be.

Food in Thai is *aharn,* and a restaurant is referred to as *rarn aharn* (food shop). Although in the main centers you will find restaurants that are used to catering to foreigners, in smaller towns they are not. So the unsuspecting gourmet who chooses an interesting looking dish from the counter may find it alarmingly fiery. (Drink lots of water or cold tea, and eat boiled rice to alleviate the scorching sensation in your mouth.)

To avoid nasty surprises you may find the following expressions useful. The word *krab* means "sir" or "madam," and is used by a man. A woman would use the word *ka.*

What is this?: *nee arai krab.*
Is it spicy?: *pet mai, krab/ka*
No, it isn't: *mai pet krab/ka*
Yes, it is spicy: *pet, krab/ka*
It's a little spicy: *pet nit noi*
It's very spicy: *pet mark*

However, visitors to Thailand who insist on eating only Western food during their stay are missing out on some gourmet delights. Also, Thai dishes usually cost far less than Western-style meals.

MEALS
Many Thais like to eat noodle soup or rice soup (*kao tom*) for breakfast (*aharn chau*), but in hotels and restaurants catering to tourists it is possible to get toast(*kanom pang pin*), jam, fruit juices, and even bacon and eggs.

Lunch (*aharn klangwan*)is usually eaten promptly at noon, or even before. It is often a fairly light meal of fried rice or noodles.

Dinner or supper (*aharn jen*) takes place from six o'clock onward. Generally speaking the Thais eat early in the evening, though special banquets may start later. Rice will be a prominent feature of the meal accompanied by a steamed dish, a fried dish, curry, soup, and salad—all taken together, not as separate courses.

These are the main meals of the day, but the Thais can be seen devouring snacks at all times, and everywhere you will find noodle sellers catering to their apparently insatiable hunger. One sometimes wonders how Thai women manage to keep their svelte figures when they spend so much of the day eating at noodle stalls!

In some traditional eating places, trays of dishes are laid out in the shop window or on the counter and you point to what you would like. Also, some of the major hotels organize buffet meals. In other places you may be presented with a menu written entirely in Thai or in Thai English, which may not be readily comprehensible, although often highly amusing. In either situation the following glossary will help.

WORDS ON THE MENU

The most common words on the Thai menu include *kai* (egg), *gai* (chicken), *moo* (pork), *nua* (beef), and *pet* (duck). Dried beef and pork have a particularly strong flavor.

Thailand is particularly renowned for its fish and seafood dishes, though if you are dining some distance from the sea, bear in mind that river fish might be fresher. Popular seafood includes *gung* (prawn), *pla* (fish), *plakapong* (sea bass, a great favorite), *plamik* (squid), *hoi* (shellfish), *hoi kreng* (cockles), *aharn taley* (seafood), and *boo* (crab).

Among the vegetables you will find *hom* (onion), *het* (mushroom), *pakad hom* (lettuce, which should be avoided unless you know it has been washed in clean water), *makeyatet*, tomatoes, and *prik* (chili). If you want food that is not too highly spiced, say, "*mai sai prik*"—"don't add chili."

TYPICAL DISHES

Thai dishes use all the ingredients specified above, to which they add various flavors, notably garlic, coriander root, black pepper, lemon grass, ginger, and chili. Here are some of the most common dishes.

Geng ped (curry), and *geng ped gai* (chicken curry). You may need to differentiate between *geng pet kiau* (green curry) and *geng pet deng* (red curry). *Geng mussaman* will be a Malay-type curry common in the extreme south of Thailand.

Geng jert is soup. Again, you need to specify. *Geng jert nua* is beef soup. It is often served in metal vessels with charcoal underneath to keep the soup hot.

Tom yam is a hot, spicy soup. This is one of the most popular dishes in Thailand, especially *tom yam gung* (spicy prawn soup).

Kau pat (fried rice) is a popular one-dish meal, and can be served with almost anything. *Kau pat moo* is pork-fried rice. Cucumber and spring onions usually accompany the dish.

Kwitiau (noodle soup) is of Chinese origin and found on many a noodle stall. It is sometimes eaten with chopsticks. *Bami* are noodles, and come in various shapes and sizes. *Bami lad na gung* is prawn cooked with noodles, and is a meal in itself. *Meekrob* (crispy noodle) is also worth trying.

Tawt man pla or *tawt man kung* (fish or prawn cakes) are interesting, chewy dishes.

Yam (salad) is much spicier than the Western type of salad, and should be sampled only by the more intrepid visitor.

Kau sooay (plain rice) is usually steamed, delightfully fluffy, and of high quality. This is the staple food of Thailand, and the Thais eat it with virtually every meal. *Kau niau* (sticky rice) is a speciality of the northeast, where it is sometimes cooked in banana leaves. Potatoes (*man farang*) do not feature in Thai cooking, being rather expensive, though they are served with Western-style food.

The following words are useful: *nerng* (steamed), *pao* (grilled), *tawt* (fried), *prioowan* (sweet and sour). When ordering, make sure you put the ingredient first and the manner of preparation second, so you get *gung tawt* (fried prawn), *pla prioowan* (sweet and sour fish).

CONDIMENTS

To add flavor to your food, should it not be tasty enough, liquid condiments are placed on the table in small saucers. They include *nam pla*, a salty brown sauce made from fermented fish; *nam pla sai prik*, fish sauce with chopped red and green chilis; and *nam prik Siracha*, Siracha sauce, which looks like tomato ketchup, but is in fact a hot chili sauce, available in several strengths. It is named after a town just north of Pattaya beach resort and is now exported. Various other sauces will appear on the table to complement other foods.

FRUIT AND DESSERTS

Thailand has a wonderful variety of fruit (*ponlamai*) including a number of exotic varieties that seldom appear in shops back home. The great luxury for Thais is *durian*, which is a large, spiky, pithy fruit that is foul smelling but treasured for its flavor. If you can't stand the smell, settle for durian ice cream instead.

Many of the delicious fruits you come across on market stalls have been freshly picked. Do not be put off by oranges with green skins: that is their natural color when ripe. You will find bananas (*glooai*), mangos (*mamuang*), papayas (*malagor*), pineapples (*saparot*), pomelo (*som o*), rambutan (*ngo*), custard apple (*noi na*), jackfruit (*kanoon*), and mangosteen (*munkut*). Strawberries, apples, and other temperate climate fruit are now being cultivated in the north of Thailand.

Coconut (*maprao*) can be bought fresh from food stands. The vendor will chop the top off and give you a straw so you can drink the juice. This is sometimes used in curry, particularly in the south, but desiccated coconut with water added is more usual in this dish.

Thai desserts (*kanom*) tend to be rather sweet, and often contain rice or coconut. Among the most common ones are *kanom maprao* (coconut cake), *glooai buat chee* (banana in coconut cream), *glooai tawt* (banana fritters), *kau niau* (sticky rice), and *sankaya fak tong* (pumpkin custard).

DRINKS

Non-Alcoholic Beverages

The Thais drink a lot of tea (*namcha*). This is usually jasmine tea and is drunk plain without milk and sugar, but you can also have tea with milk. Thailand has had tea plantations in the north of the country for over three decades. *Namcha ron* is hot tea, but it is often served with ice (*namcha yen*) in preference to plain water (*nam plau*).

Coffee is served black or with condensed milk added. Differentiate between *kafe ron* (hot coffee), *ooliang* (iced coffee), and *kafe net* (Nescafe). The last is usually more acceptable to Western taste buds. Traditional coffee is grown in the south of Thailand and is usually mixed with chicory.

Bottled water (*nam kuat*) is available in many hotels, and internationally known soft drinks are ubiquitous. Fresh lime juice (*nam manau*) is refreshing, as is orange juice (*nam som*), though you may be fobbed off with the bottled variety.

Alcoholic Beverages
Beer

Consumption of beer is growing in Thailand, but beer is heavily taxed and therefore quite expensive. Thai beer is a lager-type beer and fairly strong—normally in excess of 5 percent proof.

The most widely available beer is Singha beer from Thailand's oldest brewery, Boon Rawd. Other Thai beers are Bangkok Beer and Beer Chang (Elephant Beer). International lagers, such as Carlsberg and Heineken, are now being brewed in Thailand. Some bars sell draft beer (*bia sot*) from the barrel.

Spirits

Thai men are partial to imported whiskey and brandy, which is widely available and expensive. The cheapest form of Thai spirit is *Mekhong*, named after the river, and there is another more highly regarded local whiskey known as *Sangsom*. Currently *Black Cat*, a Thai Scotch, is popular. In country areas homemade rice wine (*kache*) is popular, but beware, as it can be potent.

Wine

Grape wines tend to be very expensive in comparison with other drinks, even those made from Thai produce. Vineyards are a relatively new feature of the landscape of the north and northeast, with *Chateau de Loei* from the northern province of Loei one of the longest established. *Maejo Red* from the

Agricultural University at Chiang Mai also has its admirers. Wines are also made from other fruit, such as mangosteen.

Finally, here are some useful words associated with drinking:

Cheers: *chaiyo*

Glass: *geo*

Bottle: *kuat*

"One more bottle": *khaw ik kuat ning krab*

Cup or dish: *tooai*

Plate: *jarn*

Milk: *nom*

"Without milk": *mai sai nom*

Sugar: *namtan*

chapter eight

GETTING ABOUT

ARRIVAL

Most visitors arrive by air at Don Muang Airport to the north of Bangkok, but not for much longer, it seems. Work is under way on a new airport to the southeast of the capital, so this information will eventually no longer apply.

If you are not being met at the airport the best idea is to catch an airport bus into Bangkok. You will find a counter at the airport selling tickets. There are three bus routes, with stops at some of the larger hotels. If there are several in your party you might consider taking an airport taxi, and again you can pay for it in advance.

There are direct international flights to some of the provincial airports, notably Chiang Mai and Phuket, which eliminate the need to change planes in Bangkok. If you come to Bangkok on the international express train from Malaysia, the terminus is Hualampong Railway station, in the middle of Bangkok, which will be on the route of the new underground railway (subway). The best plan is to get a taxi from here.

ENTRY RESTRICTIONS

Visas are not necessary for tourists staying up to thirty days. For some nationals only fifteen-day visas are available. If you plan to stay longer, you should get your visa in advance from a Thai embassy or consulate. Check www.mfa.go.th for up-to-date immigration regulations. Do not outstay the period indicated in your visa; the penalties for doing so are a fine or imprisonment.

TRANSPORT IN BANGKOK

Bangkok is a tremendously congested city and it may take longer to get to your destination than you expect by road. The new overhead mass transit railway (the Skytrain) is fast and cheap but has only a few routes so far. The city's first underground railway is due to open in 2004.

Buses

The ordinary buses are cheap but tend to get crowded and the seats are designed for petite Thais rather than large-limbed foreigners. If you want to use public transport treat yourself to an air-conditioned bus. These are a little more expensive but are usually reliable and have English-speaking bus conductors aboard. Note that the back seats of buses are reserved for monks, and if you are sitting there and a monk boards the bus you should give it up.

Taxis

Taxis are cheap—only those in Kathmandu are cheaper, according to a globe-trotting friend—but a taxi driver may refuse to take you to the destination you want at peak  times because he does not want to get stuck in a traffic jam (*rot tit,* "the cars are stuck," will be his excuse).

Hotel taxis tend to be more luxurious and more expensive. However, the hotel staff will be happy to instruct the driver precisely where to take you and this can have its advantages for the newcomer.

Three-wheeled motorized trishaws (*samlor*) with their characteristic "tuktuk" sound are cheaper than the four-wheeled taxis, but are also slower and less safe. However, they are an excellent mode of transport on the quieter roads. You usually have to negotiate a fare at the outset.

Driving a Car

This is an option for the intrepid, but many people find it is less hair-raising to drive themselves than to be driven. There are a number of good local car rental companies in Bangkok that offer more competitive rates than the multinationals, though their cars will not always be the latest models. You may prefer to hire a driver with the car, which will add only about 50 percent to the cost.

Driving is on the left—as in the U.K. and Australia—and although there is a Highway Code of sorts most drivers appear to ignore it. Be prepared to drive aggressively and let your motto be "Who dares, wins." As you are likely to spend considerable amounts of time in traffic jams, renting an air-conditioned car is advisable.

Water Transport

There is a frequent river-bus service that zigzags between the banks of the Chao Phraya River. This is faster than going by road and much more fun. If you are visiting Thailand as a tourist, it makes sense to stay at a place close to the river since transport to the main sights will be easier and more pleasurable.

Walking

You are unlikely to want to walk far on the pavements of Bangkok because of the pollution, the heat, and the humidity. However, a saunter around Sanam Luang, Lumpini Park, or some of the temple complexes is more bearable. Be careful when crossing the road; even at pedestrian crossings the traffic is unlikely to slow down to let you cross.

TRANSPORT IN THE PROVINCES

Air
The national carrier, Thai Airways, operates scheduled services to all the main centers, and a few private airlines are now springing up, such as Bangkok Air. If you are in a hurry to get around this must be your transport of choice.

Train
This is a good, and safe, way to see the country. Train services run from Bangkok to Chiang Mai, Nongkai, and Ubon in the northeast, Aranya Prathet in the east, Pattaya to the southeast, Kanchanaburi in the west, and via Haadyai in the south to Kuala Lumpur and Singapore. There are three classes of travel, and there are overnight trains with sleepers (bookable in advance) on some long-distance routes. Supplements are payable for certain trains, sleepers, and

air-conditioning. Charges are listed on the Thai
Railways Web site (www.railway.co.th).

Most of the Thai railway system is single-
track and the trains tend to amble—no
Japanese-style bullet trains here! But it looks as if
that is all set to change. As this book goes to
press the state-owned company is inviting bids
for a high-speed railway line of standard
gauge—as opposed to the present meter gauge.
In ten years' time perhaps one will no longer be
able to categorize Thai trains as "slow, slower,
and slowest." Diesel railcars, which tend to be
third-class only and with limited legroom, can
be faster than the so-called express trains.

Bus

This is the cheapest way to get about, but some of
the bus drivers tend to be erratic. The state BKS
bus company (known as "Baw Kaw Saw") runs
long-distance orange buses to all parts of the
country from the three bus stations in Bangkok.

Air-conditioned long-distance buses run to
some towns, and local tour companies run
bus services to resorts that can pick you up at
your hotel. Both of these options are more
expensive. For really long distances, such as
Bangkok to Chiang Mai, bus travel is not to be
recommended; train and air travel are more
comfortable.

In each province local bus companies ply short-distance routes. If you are on the large side you may have trouble fitting into the seats.

Thai bus drivers (like truck drivers) are a law unto themselves and drive fast and with little regard for other users of the road. In the event of an accident, it is not unknown for the driver to flee the scene.

Taxis

In provincial towns you will find taxis to hire, but in the smaller towns pedicabs and motorized trishaws (*samlors*) are often a better bet, but you need to negotiate the fare in advance. Out of town you may find shared taxis (*sengteo*) a convenient way of

getting around. These are usually small pickup trucks with seats in the back that ply regular routes and are fairly frequent. Fares are cheap and there is no need to haggle.

Driving Yourself

This is a good way of getting around as Thailand has an excellent network of well-maintained main roads, some of them expressways, and traffic jams are rare in the provinces. If renting a car, make sure the rental charge includes insurance, since Thai driving is erratic and many drivers seem to be oblivious to other traffic on the road. Gasoline is only lightly taxed and therefore remarkably cheap by European standards. If you are involved in an accident, it is advisable to drive straight to the nearest police station rather than become involved in a discussion. At beach resorts motorcycle and bicycle rentals are available.

Water Transport
Long-tailed boats (motorized) operate along the extensive canal network of the central plain and the rivers.

It is sensible to avoid traveling during public holidays, especially the Songkhran festival in April, when public transport is overstretched and the nation's roads are jam-packed. The road accident statistics soar at Songkhran.

WHERE TO STAY
This is not a problem. Bangkok is well supplied with hotels and guesthouses to suit every budget and virtually every provincial capital has at least one smart, modern hotel with air-conditioned rooms and much more besides. Even in the smallest townships you will find Chinese hotels—possibly built of wood, with ceiling fans and windows with netting designed to keep out the

mosquitoes. They are basic but normally clean and tremendously good value.

Although most people book accommodation through a travel agent, there are excellent Web sites with details of hotel accommodation (though not the rock-bottom cheapest) throughout the country. Try www.thaihotels.com or www.stayinthailand.com. Since the supply of hotel rooms greatly outstrips demand, except at holiday times, there is little need to book in advance. Just turn up and be prepared to bargain.

SECURITY
Thailand is no worse than any other country when it comes to crime, which means you should not be lulled into a false sense of security. Handbags get snatched, pockets get picked, cars get burgled, and baggage gets stolen if left unattended, so you need to take reasonable precautions, especially in the main tourist spots.

The Thais are particularly anxious that foreign visitors should go away with a good impression of the country—after all, tourism is a big moneymaker for them—so they now employ tourist police in most of the areas where visitors go.

Women are not particularly at risk in Thailand. Generally speaking, foreign women are treated with politeness and respect, and Thais will often compliment you on your fair skin and your gorgeous hair. But beware of behaving in an over-friendly manner with Thai men in case your motives are misconstrued.

Men, on the other hand, may get pestered by pimps after dark offering them all manner of sexual services with such blandishments as *"Mister ow puying mai?"* (Would you like a girl?) A firm *"mai ow, krab"* (No, thanks) should be a sufficient deterrent, but if they persist, complain to the tourist police.

HEALTH MATTERS

Rumors of people dying of dengue fever, malaria, diarrhea, food poisoning, and so on are greatly exaggerated. Provided you behave sensibly you can avoid illness. Before setting out, read official government health advice for travelers regarding any vaccinations that may be necessary, and other practical information. No vaccinations are obligatory unless you are coming from a disease-ridden part of the world.

Arm yourself with medicines to relieve indigestion, diarrhea, dysentery, headaches, and travel sickness. Antiseptic cream, plasters, and insect repellent are also recommended. These can be obtained in any Thai pharmacy.

Don't spend too much time in the sun. It is very strong, especially around midday. Wear a hat or sit in the shade. Sunglasses are a must.

Drink a lot, or you will become dehydrated, but take care what you drink. Don't drink from mountain springs, the river, or stagnant pools. Bottled water is best, and if you don't like sugary mineral waters, ask for soda water. Always take more salt than you would in a temperate climate.

Eat only cooked food. Salads should be eaten only where you know for certain that the ingredients have been washed in clean water.

When sitting outside in the evening use insect repellent. Thai mosquitoes do not carry malaria (except in some border areas), but they do bite. Most bedrooms have netting at the windows to keep them out, with varying degrees of success. If camping out, a mosquito net is essential equipment.

Slow down. Take it easy, like the Thais. If you dash about trying to fit everything in as you might in a temperate climate, you will suffer headaches or tiredness. Don't expect to achieve as much as you would in a temperate climate.

If you experience a skin rash where clothes rub against the skin, prickly heat powder should relieve it.

Exercise great care in sexual matters. If you indulge, there is a risk of contracting AIDS, gonorrhea, and other sexually transmitted diseases. If you believe you are infected, see a doctor immediately. Embassies and consulates can advise on medical facilities, but most clinics have experience in dealing with such diseases.

Culture shock is another problem to be aware of! Some visitors suffer from imaginary ailments and phobias, the cause of which can be put down to feelings of alienation in strange surroundings. But most people get over this problem. If you have digested the information in this book carefully and acted on it, such a situation need not arise.

chapter nine

BUSINESS BRIEFING

Not so long ago Thailand was regarded as a Third World country, exporting mainly primary products—such as timber, rice, handicrafts, gems—and importing most of the manufactured goods it needed. Over the past three or four decades, however, manufacturing has taken off in a big way and the country is now regarded as a Newly Industrialized Country (NIC).

In the early nineties Thailand boasted the fastest growing economy in the world, and foreign businessmen led by the Japanese were lining up to invest in the country. Today manufacturing accounts for 34.5 percent of the country's output as opposed to agriculture, which is down to 11.5 percent. The service sector, led by tourism, accounts for 46 percent.

The good times were too good to last, and in 1997 boom turned to bust. Thai investors overborrowed to finance lavish construction projects and then everything turned sour. Businesses and banks went bankrupt; millionaires became paupers overnight; the Thai *baht*, once regarded as a strong currency, plummeted in value; and the country had to turn to the International Monetary Fund for assistance.

Fortunately those dark days appear to be over. The Thai economy appears to have stabilized and the shoots of recovery have appeared. Thailand is open for business again.

PREPARATION IS VITAL

While the overwhelming majority of visitors to Thailand come as tourists, around 9.5 million in 2002, an appreciable number—over 800,000 per annum—come for professional reasons: to sell, to invest, to set up a business, to offer aid, to advise, to write about the country, to lecture, and so on. If you fall into this category you arrive with certain objectives in mind, and you naturally hope that your efforts will be successful.

Success cannot always be guaranteed. Some visitors fail spectacularly to achieve their aims and retire frustrated from the fray, blaming the Thais for being uncooperative, devious, impossible, and closed to new ideas. Yet most of the blame probably lies not with the Thais but with the way the visitors have conducted themselves; they have not taken into account local attitudes and customs and have failed to adapt accordingly.

Nearly every foreigner arriving in Thailand suffers from a built-in disadvantage. The Thais you will meet will know more about you and the way you operate than you do about them. If you want to find out who's who in the Premier Division of U.K. football, you cannot do better than ask a Thai.

This should come as no surprise. Thailand has been trading with a diversity of countries since the seventeenth century and, unlike its neighbors in the region that were colonized, has always been able to pick and choose its trading partners. As a result the Thais are sophisticated negotiators even when they appear to be negotiating from a position of weakness, as has happened on several occasions in their turbulent history.

Moreover, a surprisingly large number of Thais, especially the younger ones, will have studied abroad—in the U.S.A., Australia, New Zealand, Europe, and elsewhere in Asia. But that does not mean that they have abandoned their own values and way of life in favor of foreign lifestyles and attitudes.

There is no excuse for arriving in Thailand in a state of ignorance, especially since

there are a number of organizations that can offer you advice. Several countries have a chamber of commerce in Bangkok, and if you are a prospective investor there are a number of government and private Web sites offering information, e.g., www.boi.or.th. Do not overlook the various briefing organizations in your own country that can advise you on how to proceed.

THE CHINESE IN BUSINESS

When is a Chinese not a Chinese? When he's a Thai. In some countries of southeast Asia, such as Malaysia and Indonesia, the Chinese are a race apart, but in Thailand this is no longer the case. There has been a great deal of intermarriage, and most Chinese have adopted Thai names and ways.

This is perhaps not so surprising. Many of them were born here, have Thai nationality, and regard Thailand as their home. Some are perhaps less well integrated than others, and there are Thais who envy them their wealth and domination of the business sector, but on the whole there is little, if any, racial tension.

You sometimes gather the impression that the Chinese are striving to be more Thai than the Thais themselves. Certainly Chinese visitors from Hong Kong or Beijing might regard them as different, despite the fact that like Chinese everywhere, they are proud of their roots and place a high premium on entrepreneurship, hard work, education, and training.

In matters of commerce they are preeminent. It is estimated that just thirty Chinese families have interests in over eight hundred Thai companies. For this reason it pays to be cautious in your business dealings. Playing off one company against another could be risky when there is a strong

likelihood that the other firm is owned by a close relation of the person you are negotiating with.

The Chinese have a keen sense of fun and their gambling instinct means they are willing to take risks. There is no doubt that their commercial dynamism is a contributory factor to Thailand's remarkable economic progress. In the past Thai monarchs relied on them to provide the country's commercial infrastructure, while the Thais themselves preferred to work on the land or in government.

Thai society is now in a state of flux. The ethnic Thais no longer shun commerce, and you will now find Chinese active in politics and government. Some Thai companies and organizations are starting to develop a culture of their own that may differ in some respects from the norms described below, and visitors will need to watch out for such differences.

By no means are all the long-established companies in Thailand Chinese. There is one interesting historical reminder. If you go along Siphya Road in Bangkok you will come across the firm of Louis T. Leonowens Ltd., the name of which has a familiar ring. It was founded by Louis, the son of Anna Leonowens, who came to Siam in 1862 at the invitation of King Mongkut to teach the royal children. Louis attended his mother's lessons at the palace, where one of his fellow pupils was a prince who would later become the much-revered King Chulalongkorn. After completing his education in England, Louis returned to Siam and became a captain in the King's army. This led to a border surveying and protection assignment in the timber areas of the north where he was to make his fortune as a pioneer in the Siamese teak industry.

He started his own business in 1896, and his trading company Louis T. Leonowens Ltd. was registered in Bangkok at the beginning of the twentieth century. Although the company is now owned by Getz Bros & Co., Inc., it keeps the Leonowens name alive to this day.

MANAGEMENT THAI STYLE

If you are dealing with Thai companies or have set up a company in Thailand, do not assume that these companies are run in the same way that they would be back home. In the West people work for a company or organization, and their loyalty is to that organization. In Thailand organizations are not run collectively, as in Japan, but by one person. That person has to be someone able to exercise authority and who can command respect. The older and more important he (or she) is, the more he (or she) will be respected. Thai workers are loyal to their boss, provided he does all that is required of him.

However, a manager's role is not confined to achieving work targets. It spills over into other areas. In Thai society superiors have obligations to the people in their charge. They are expected to treat them kindly, paying attention to their welfare, and covering up their mistakes. A manager is regarded as a patron by his staff, and is expected to empathize with them and assist them in all kinds of ways, from helping their relatives find jobs to presiding over weddings.

This entails performing a balancing act between the exercise of authority (*pradet*) and patronage (*prakun*). If you look after your staff well, you will earn their respect and loyalty, and they will be prepared to go that extra mile for you when you need it. But if you fail to develop a deep and trusting relationship with your subordinates, your position is weakened.

In Western companies it is usual practice to fire staff if they are not performing well. Not so in Thai companies, where most employees expect to spend all their lives in the same company. To dismiss someone for incompetence or laziness could cause them to lose face. Besides, they may have powerful contacts. If you need to reprove someone, tread very carefully. Praise is a far more potent motivator than blame.

Some international companies with subsidiaries operating in Thailand have been known to bite the bullet and fire the local manager, but actions like this can have unintended, and unfortunate, consequences.

ESTABLISHING TRUST

The Thais prefer do to business with someone they know and trust, so your priority must be to establish a good working relationship (*nam jai*). This inevitably takes time, so patience is essential. Nobody should expect to arrive in Bangkok one day and leave with a contract signed, sealed, and delivered the next.

First impressions are important, which is why you should abide strictly by the dress code, especially in Bangkok. You might imagine that in view of the capital's hot and sticky climate people would dress down for comfort, but you would be wrong. Thai men dress in smart suits for formal meetings and visits, and they expect visitors to do the same. Thai women look equally smart. Blame this all on the former Thai Prime Minister Phibul Songkhram for insisting that formal Western dress was a mark of civilization, and anything else was not.

To make life bearable you might want to invest at the outset in a custom-made lightweight suit, which a local Indian or Chinese tailor should be able to run up for you in twenty-four hours as you recover from jet lag. Bear in mind, too, that many of the buildings you will be visiting have superefficient air-conditioning.

For informal gatherings outside business hours more casual attire is often worn, provided it looks smart. Brightly colored Thai cotton or silk shirts go over very well on these occasions, but it is wise to check what the dress code will be to avoid embarrassment. It goes without saying that you should be well groomed and, ideally, clean-shaven. The Thais distrust people with beards and unkempt hair.

Do not underestimate the importance of social gatherings, as this is one way of gaining trust. Also, while eating your noodles you may well learn useful snippets of information that do not come out during the formal meetings. Thais who are inhibited about voicing their opinions in formal meetings because of their lack of fluency in English are more likely to open up in a more relaxed atmosphere.

So be prepared to brush up your social skills and realize that time spent making small talk in good company is often time well spent. However, avoid becoming so relaxed that you forget the rules of etiquette; steer away from taboo subjects, and don't make jokes that are liable to be lost in translation. Remember that a certain amount of flattery always goes over well.

MEETINGS

Some visitors set themselves a tight schedule on the assumption that they can cram in several meetings in one day. In Bangkok, where most meetings are likely to take place, this is frankly unrealistic. If the meetings are at different locations, you will have to allow plenty of time to get from one place to the next. Furthermore,  the meetings will take longer than you expect if you are working through an interpreter.

Another factor you need to consider is the timing of a meeting. A twelve o'clock meeting is definitely out, as this is when the Thais stop for lunch. Some are unlikely to resume work much before 2:00 p.m. In government offices officials start leaving before the end of the afternoon. Don't be surprised if a rendezvous at 8:30 a.m. is suggested, since this is when many people arrive at their desks.

As far as business and official meetings are concerned, punctuality is important. If you are expected at a place at a certain time, it is bad form to arrive late, whatever your excuse.

Meetings tend to be formal affairs, involving a number of people although some of them will say very little. Brainstorming sessions seldom work as the Thais have been brought up in an educational tradition where one is discouraged from speaking out. Besides, if they propose an idea that could be flawed, or just plain wrong, they could lose face. Even if they have a sound idea, junior staff may prefer not to air it in public out of deference to their superiors.

They will listen respectfully to what you have to say and there may be some pauses for interpretation and for discussion in Thai or Chinese (usually the southern Chinese Teochiu dialect). People will smile and nod as if in agreement—though you should not assume that they do see eye to eye—and the meeting may be terminated without coming to any conclusion. This is not necessarily a bad omen.

It is important to look for clues as to the identity of the key player or decision-maker during the meeting, particularly if this is not made clear from the start. It is likely to be an older rather than a younger person, since in Thailand organizations tend to be hierarchical. Sometimes this is not always obvious, as another member of the staff may handle much of the discussion while his boss looks on.

You may get a clue from the business card you are given at the outset, which will detail a person's rank and title. Meetings usually start off with an exchange of business cards, and you should always have a good stock of your own at hand, which indicate your qualifications and your status within your organization. At one time it was customary to have cards with details printed in English on one side and Thai on the other, but this is no longer necessary.

If you are still not clear as to who the decision-maker is, observe the body language carefully. The others will treat him (it is usually a man) with deference, and they will always agree with his pronouncements. Harmony is always maintained in meetings. If someone enters the room they will look toward him and either *wai* or stoop.

Even if the meeting is conducted in a relaxed manner, do not assume that you can forget the rules of Thai etiquette. You need to be polite, speak in a quiet voice, and not get too worked up. In other words, be cool, calm, and collected—and make sure you do not commit any *faux pas.*

> *An American investment banker was getting on well with the Thai Director of Finance in a government ministry. As he relaxed, the American leaned back in his chair and crossed his legs, exposing the soles of his feet. His lack of finesse shocked the Thai, who politely made his excuses and quickly brought the meeting to an end. There was no contact between the ministry and the banker for a full year.*

DEALING WITH THE GOVERNMENT

Senior government officials have a high status in Thai society, and should always be treated with a measure of deference. But bear in mind that many of the people in the top jobs will be political appointees who will often delegate decisions to permanent civil servants. These are the people of real significance, and it is important to forge as strong a relationship as possible with them since their cooperation will be crucial.

The government often calls in consultants and other experts to offer advice on a short-term basis—even though it has a highly educated cadre of civil servants who are only too aware of what needs to be done. Unfortunately, because of the hierarchical nature of the civil service, younger civil servants tend not to voice their opinions for fear of antagonizing others further up the chain of command. Promotion depends on the extent to which you toe the line, though this may no longer be true of every branch of government.

Knowing Best

A senior official of the Ministry of Education once confided to me that they had had a stream of education advisers—they all came as part of an aid package—but it was difficult to act on their advice since one adviser tended to put forward ideas that contradicted those of his predecessor. Few of them really addressed the country's educational needs.

How could they? They knew virtually nothing about the Thai educational system and were trying to graft on methods that had worked elsewhere, but were not really appropriate to Thai conditions.

A foreign consultant starts with a built-in advantage. People in authority are more likely to listen to his (or her) views, even if they eventually decide not to take the advice offered. But the expert is sometimes hampered by a lack of local knowledge. Management theories that work well elsewhere may be nonstarters in Thailand because of the very different culture that operates.

The best plan is to arrive without preconceived notions and to begin by soliciting the views of people who are close to the action. If their status is fairly junior, they may never have been asked their views by their superiors. The place to hear their ideas is not in the large set-piece meetings where they will tend to keep quiet, but at a more informal level—over a bowl of *kwitiau*, for instance.

Often their ideas may prove useful, and you may well be able to incorporate them into the report without incurring any resentment. They will be flattered that you have found their suggestions worthwhile and pleased that they form part of your recommendations.

Thai civil servants are not particularly well paid, and often have second jobs. Do not expect them to work unpaid overtime in order to help you.

The Foreign Expert

Not all consultants are so highly regarded. A British businessman was in a meeting at a government ministry with a group of Thais and one lone Westerner who seemed rather quiet and ill at ease. The businessman felt he ought to draw this fellow-Westerner into the discussion and began to address some remarks to him—at which the chairman of the meeting interjected, "Don't worry about him. He's only our expert."

KICKBACKS

Corruption seems to be endemic in many parts of the Orient, and Thailand is not immune to such practices, though it is by no means the worst offender.

In the past it was customary for a Chinese businessman to receive protection from influential

Thais in return for payments; in the early sixties Prime Minister General Sarit is alleged to have diverted 140 million *baht* from public funds into his own bank account, and a recent study revealed that 75 percent of Thai MPs received commissions from development projects in their constituencies.

One question that preoccupies many a newcomer is whether one should be prepared to grease any palms in order to achieve one's objectives. It is difficult to provide a satisfactory answer. As a foreigner you should steer clear of passing brown envelopes under the table during negotiations. Such actions are unlikely to smooth the way and could land you in deep trouble if you are bidding for a government contract and the Counter Corruption Commission comes to hear of your activities.

The best solution is to find a reputable agent who can handle any payments that need to be made. If you try to do this yourself, you will invariably get it wrong. Every organization operating in Thailand—whether local or foreign—has its own Mr., Mrs., or Miss Fixit who has good contacts and knows exactly what to do to make the wheels run smoothly.

The problem of corruption is regularly aired in Thailand, and attempts have been made to combat political corruption, in particular. At a recent election some of the contests had to be rerun because they were shown to have been rigged. Also, some of the country's more perspicacious leaders realize that foreign investors may shy away from countries that are institutionally corrupt.

One reassuring piece of advice comes from a former British Ambassador to Thailand. "You should also know that some of the most successful Western firms in Bangkok have never ever resorted to illegal payments precisely because there are so many legal ways in which these delicate matters can be resolved to everyone's mutual satisfaction."

chapter ten

LANGUAGE &
COMMUNICATION

Thailand boasts a modern communications infrastructure. The postal service is efficient, as is the telephone network, and the country is one of the leading users in Asia of cell phones and the Internet. Many businesses, government departments, media organizations, and academic institutions have well-organized Web sites in both Thai and English. Internet cafés are becoming common, and most hotels and businesses have fax facilities.

MEDIA

Thailand has two English-language daily newspapers, the *Bangkok Post* and *The Nation*, and a few provincial towns now boast English-language weeklies.

There are several TV channels, both state and private, broadcasting in Thai, but you can get an English soundtrack to some programs by tuning in to certain radio stations. English-language TV programs are also beamed in by satellite and most hotels have facilities for receiving them. The BBC World Service, Voice of America, and Australian Broadcasting Corporation broadcasts can be heard on shortwave radios.

By Asian standards the Thai press is relatively free to express its own opinions and recent government attempts to muzzle it have been unsuccessful. Broadcasting tends to toe the government line; TV stations are either owned by the government or the current Prime Minister's family!

However, a good communications infrastructure is no guarantee of trouble-free communication. This chapter offers advice on how to interact successfully with Thais.

ENGLISH IN THAILAND

A few decades ago, although English was taught in schools, most Thais had few opportunities to practice their oral skills unless they went to study abroad. They learned to write it and read it, but not to speak it.

In the 1960s English received a boost with the arrival of large numbers of Westerners, notably the American military, which had bases in Thailand and used Thailand as an R & R (rest and recreation) center for soldiers fighting in Vietnam. English received a further boost as

Thailand became a popular tourist destination and a regional center for commerce and international organizations. Another significant factor is the growing number of foreign residents.

Nowadays in Bangkok and the major tourist spots English is widely spoken, along with other foreign languages, to a lesser extent. However, some of the English you come across is fairly rudimentary and not always comprehensible. In the more rural areas—"upcountry," as Thais refer to it—English ceases to be a *lingua franca*. It is not a second language in the same way as it is in Malaysia, India, and Singapore, or as French used to be in Cambodia, Laos, and Vietnam.

MAKING YOURSELF UNDERSTOOD

Misunderstandings occur frequently in Thailand, and you can never expect that your words will be immediately understood. If you see a puzzled expression on the face of the person addressed, try to express yourself more simply; try speaking more slowly (but not too slowly), quietly, and without any intonation. The Thais are more likely to comprehend what you are saying if you do not use a lot of intonation in your speech.

When using taxis, the best idea is to ask a Thai to write your destination down in Thai for you. Failing that, write it down in English; and give it to the taxi driver. Thailand boasts a high standard of literacy (95 percent of the adult population) and most people in the travel and tourist trades seem to be able to read Thai and English.

Mixed Messages

A visiting American academic was invited to give a lecture in Bangkok. He summoned a taxi and told the driver his destination. The driver beamed at him, and a few minutes later stopped outside a massage parlor, much to the lecturer's astonishment. He had asked to be driven to Thammasart (the university). The driver thought he had said "To massage!"

UNDERSTANDING THAI ENGLISH

Just as foreigners experience difficulties communicating in Thai, they may also have problems in coping with English as spoken by Thais, especially the less well educated. Thais have some major pronunciation difficulties.

Thais often separate consonants by inserting a vowel between them: "whiskey" becomes "wisiki," and smart becomes "semart." Sometimes they drop a consonant: "excuse me" becomes "sku me." Some word endings are difficult for Thais, apart from the endings "m," "n," "ng," or "t." With words ending in "l" the final consonant is often pronounced "n," so you'll hear "bin" for "bill" and "Hoten Orienten" for Hotel Oriental. In words ending in the sounds "s," "sh," "ch," "j," and "th" the final consonant is pronounced "t." Sandwich becomes "senwit," "wash" becomes "wot," and Smith becomes "Samit." And in Bangkok Thai, in particular, "r" may be pronounced as "l," as in "collect" instead of "correct," "light" instead of "right," or may be omitted altogether.

Grammatically, the Thais often transfer the rules of their own language to English. For example, pronouns are often omitted if it is obvious who is being referred to. The present tense is used even when referring to the past or future if the context is clear (I see him yesterday). No distinction is normally made between singular and plural. There is no definite or indefinite article. The verb "to be" is omitted.

Many Thais know more English than they care to let on, but are hesitant to speak it for fear of making mistakes and thereby losing face. So if a Thai is speaking to you in English, listen carefully and encouragingly and they will become more relaxed.

LEARNING THAI

There are many advantages to being able to speak Thai, even at a rudimentary level. For one thing the

Thais will appreciate your making the effort, even if they giggle at your pronunciation. Moreover, some knowledge of the language will help you to bargain more effectively in shops and at markets, and to find your way around. For, while you may be able to get by with English in the main centers, once off the beaten track you may find yourself among people who have no notion of English whatsoever.

There are Thai language courses in many Western countries. For books and CDs try the Web site www.thailanguage.com. In Thailand itself there are also courses. One of the best-known is held at the AUA Center in Bangkok.

Pronunciation Matters

In an upcountry restaurant not all that far from Bangkok, an Englishman decided to order sea bass (*plakapong*), and sat back looking forward with relish to this Thai speciality. Unfortunately his pronunciation was slightly awry, and instead of a dish of delicious fish steamed in ginger and herbs he was served with a plate of sardines. The waitress had thought he wanted tinned fish (*plakrapong*).

The main problem for most foreigners—with the exception of the Chinese and Vietnamese—is that the Thai language is tonal. That means that words are differentiated not only by the vowels and consonants but also the tone—which can be flat, high, low, rising, or falling.

Take the word *kau*, for instance. It can mean news, white, rice, mountain, or he/she/it, depending on the tone employed. The word pretty is pronounced *sooai*, but if you are complimenting a girl you must pronounce it correctly, otherwise it will mean bad luck. And perfectly innocuous words can be rude ones if you use the wrong tone!

We do employ tones in English, only we call it intonation. For instance, a question ends on a rising tone, and its answer would end on a falling tone. We do not have a high tone or a low tone in English, so you may need to enlist the help of a Thai to demonstrate it to you—you could start by asking them to pronounce the numerals 1-10: *ning, song, sam, see, ha, hok, jet, bat, gao, sip*. The level (or mid) tone is fairly easy to achieve if you model your pronunciation on that of the robot R2D2 in *Star Wars*.

Take away the tones, and Thai would not be a difficult language to pronounce.

If you are planning to stay in Thailand for any length of time you will find it useful to learn to read and write Thai, but for everyday purposes it is advisable to learn to speak it first.

ADDRESSING PEOPLE IN THAI

When addressing people the safest way is to preface their first name by *khun,* which means Mr., Mrs., or Miss. So you would address Chuan Vongsiri as *khun* Chuan. The Thais may call you by your first name in English—Mr. Bill—rather than by your surname—Mr. Smith. When asking a person's name the normal expression is *khun chur arai, krab (or ka)*?

If a person has a royal title (and if you are on an official visit you may well meet such a person) it is advisable to find out in advance how to address him or her, and in some cases you will be presented with a card giving all the relevant details. However, it is perfectly in order to address a person, even the prime minister, as *khun.*

The Thais use a polite term at the end of practically every sentence. If you are a man, it is *krab* and if a woman, *ka.* For example, to say "hello" or "good day" in Thai (which is *sawat dee*) a man would say *sawat dee krab* and a woman *sawat dee ka.* If speaking to a child, you would say *sawat dee noo.* Women often substitute the word *ca* when addressing friends.

A WORD ABOUT TIME

The way the Thais refer to time can be confusing to a foreigner. They divide the day into seven parts: 1:00 a.m. to 6:00 a.m. (*tee ning, tee song, tee sam, tee see, tee ha, tee hok*); 7:00 a.m. to 11:00 a.m. (*mong chau, song mong chau, sam mong chau, see mong chau, ha mong chau*); noon (*tian klangwan*); 1:00 p.m. to 3:00 p.m. (*bai mong, bai song mong, bai sam mong*); 4:00 p.m. to 6:00 p.m. (*mong yen, song mong yen, sam mong yen*); 7:00 p.m. to 11:00 pm (*tum, song tum, sam tum, see tum, ha tum*); midnight (*tian kern*). Minutes (*natee*) are put after the hour, so ten past midnight is *tien kern sip natee*. Half past midnight is *tian kern krung* (half).

So when you are fixing a time for a meeting, make sure you know exactly what time is being referred to. You might like to try using the 24-hour system used by Thai Railways—for example *sip si nalika*, or 1400 hours, to denote 2:00 p.m.

DOS AND DON'TS

The purpose of this book has been to enable you to interpret Thai behavior, from an understanding of the cultural values that motivate it, and to give you a feel for what constitutes appropriate behavior in this Land of Smiles. The following list is designed to remind you of the more important features of Thai etiquette, and ensure that your relations with the people remain trouble-free and cordial.

Do

Avoid close contact.

Be polite.

Dress smartly and conservatively.

Flatter and praise.

Keep your cool.

Show respect for monks and the King.

Smile and be patient.

Speak gently and clearly.

Take off your shoes when entering a
house or temple.

Use first names, preceded by *khun*.

Don't

Don't be sarcastic.

Don't moan or criticize.

Don't cross your legs.

Don't gesticulate wildly.

Don't get annoyed.

Don't point at people.

Don't point with your feet.

Don't shout.

Don't touch people's heads.

CONCLUSION

A British diplomat, W.A.R. Wood, who came to
Thailand as a young man in the last century, wrote a
book entitled *Consul in Paradise*. He eventually settled

down in this "paradise" like countless other foreigners who fall in love with the country and its people.

After the rapid industrialization of recent years, there are fears that Thailand may soon become a "paradise lost." Bangkok is no longer the tranquil city of canals that it was when Wood first came, and today one has to travel for hours from the capital to find quiet, secluded beaches.

The changes have not been all bad, however. While the Thais want to keep up their old traditions they have never hesitated to embrace the new, taking on board the latest ideas, the latest technology, and the latest fashions.

It is heartening to see that the new prosperity is reaching into the far-flung corners of the Kingdom, with the result that the once marginal hill tribes, for instance, have become successful market gardeners, and are also to be found in the main tourist centers selling the handicrafts they have made.

Modernization causes stresses and strains in any society, but there are signs that Thai society is more resilient than most. Time will tell whether the Thai character is strong enough to continue to fend off the uncouth elements of more dominant, invasive cultures and preserve the charm and gentleness of its own.

Further Reading

Coedès, George. *The Indianised States of South East Asia.*
Honolulu: East West Centre Press, 1968.

Cooper, Robert and Nanthapa. *Culture Shock! Thailand.*
Portland, Oregon: Graphic Arts Center Publishing, 2000/London:
Kuperard, 2003.

Cooper, Robert G. *Thais Mean Business: The Foreign Businessman's Guide to
Doing Business in Thailand.* Singapore and Kuala Lumpur:
Time Books International, 1992.

Cummings, Joe, Martin, and Steven. *Thailand.*
Melbourne and London: Lonely Planet, 2003.

Cummings, Joe. *World Food, Thailand.* Melbourne and London:
Lonely Planet, 2003.

Eliot, Joshua, and Janie Bickersteth. *Thailand Handbook.*
Bath: Footprint, 2001.

Eliot, Joshua, and Janie Bickersteth. *Bangkok and the Beaches Handbook.*
Bath: Footprint, 2000.

Gray, Paul, and Lucy Ridout. *Rough Guide to Thailand.*
London: Rough Guides, 2001.

Holmes, Henry, with Suchada Tantongtavy. *Working with Thais.* Bangkok:
White Lotus, 1997. (www.thailine.com/lotus)

Jumsai, Manich (M.L.). *A Popular History of Thailand.*
Bangkok: Chalermnit, 1993. (www.chalermnit.com)

Klausner, William J. *Reflections on Thai Culture.* Bangkok:
Siam Society, 1987.

Moore, John, and Saowalak Rudchue. *Colloquial Thai:
A Complete Language Course.* London: Routledge, 1994.

Phongpaichit, Pasuk, and Sunsidh Piriyarangsan.
Corruption and Democracy in Thailand. Chiang Mai: Silkworm Books,
1996. (www.silkwormbooks.com)

Phongpaichit, Pasuk, and Chris Baker. *Thailand—Economy and Politics.*
Kuala Lumpur and Oxford: Oxford University Press S.E. Asia, 1995.

Toews, Bea, and Robert McGregor. *Succeed in Business—Thailand.*
Singapore and Kuala Lumpur: Times Books International, 1998.

Thai Phrase Book and Dictionary. Oxford: Berlitz, 1994.

Van Beek, Steve, and Luca Invernizzi Tettoni. *The Arts of Thailand.* London:
Thames and Hudson, 1991.

Index

Acknowledgment

I would like to take this opportunity to record my profound gratitude to those people who have offered me insights into the Thai character, notably Denis and Chamaiporn Mulliner, Lawan and Mike Long, Gerald Owen, and Suratin Bunnag, now sadly deceased.